Cyrus Adler, I. M. Casanowicz

Biblical antiquities

A Description of the Exhibit at the Cotton States International eExposition, Atlanta, 1895

Cyrus Adler, I. M. Casanowicz

Biblical antiquities
A Description of the Exhibit at the Cotton States International eExposition, Atlanta, 1895

ISBN/EAN: 9783743419346

Manufactured in Europe, USA, Canada, Australia, Japa

Cover: Foto ©Lupo / pixelio.de

Manufactured and distributed by brebook publishing software (www.brebook.com)

Cyrus Adler, I. M. Casanowicz

Biblical antiquities

SMITHSONIAN INSTITUTION.
UNITED STATES NATIONAL MUSEUM.

BIBLICAL ANTIQUITIES.

A DESCRIPTION OF THE EXHIBIT AT THE COTTON STATES INTERNATIONAL EXPOSITION, ATLANTA, 1895.

BY

CYRUS ADLER, PH. D.,
Custodian, Section of Historic Religious Ceremonials, U. S. National Museum,

and

I. M. CASANOWICZ, PH. D.,
Aid, Division of Historic Archæology, U. S. National Museum.

From the Report of the U. S. National Museum for 1896, pages 943-1023, with forty-six plates.

WASHINGTON:
GOVERNMENT PRINTING OFFICE.
1898.

BIBLICAL ANTIQUITIES.

A DESCRIPTION OF THE EXHIBIT AT THE COTTON STATES INTERNATIONAL EXPOSITION, ATLANTA, 1895.

BY

CYRUS ADLER, PH. D.,
Custodian, Section of Historic Religious Ceremonials, U. S. National Museum,

AND

I. M. CASANOWICZ, PH. D.,
Aid, Division of Historic Archæology, U. S. National Museum.

TABLE OF CONTENTS.

	Page.
Introduction	953
The land of the Bible	953
Map of Palestine	953
Geology	954
Dust from Jerusalem	954
Water from the Jordan	954
Small shell from Tyre	954
Granite from Jebel Musa	955
Flora	955
Seed pods of the Carob tree	955
Sycamore from Palestine	955
Apples of Sodom	956
Unripe pomegranate from Palestine	956
Cone of the cedar of Lebanon	957
Cone of a Lebanon fir	958
Fauna	958
Mammals	958
The ape	958
The bat	958
"Coney"-rock-badger	959
Young camel	959
Gazelle	960
Mouse	960
Birds	960
The cock	960
Turtledove	961
Golden eagle	961
Hoopoe	962
Owl	962
Partridge	963
Peacock	963
Pelican	963
Quail	963
Raven	963
Sparrow	964
Black stork	964
Swallow	965
Griffon vulture	965
Reptiles	965
Frog	965
Lizards	965
Viper	966
Insects	966
Horsefly	966
Breeze flies	966
Sacred scarabaeus	967
Hornet	967
Locust	967
Moth	967

	Page.
Palestinian antiquities	968
Cast of the Moabite stone	968
Cast of the Siloam inscription	969
Cast of the Lachish tablet	971
Cast of the seal of Haggai, son of Shebaniah	971
Biblical weights	972
Cast of an ancient Hebrew weight	972
Cast of a bead	972
Musical instruments	973
I. Instruments of percussion	975
1. Round tabret, hand-drum	975
2. Four-sided tabret	975
3. Kettledrum	975
4. Cymbals	975
5. Castanets	976
II. Wind instruments	976
1. Ram's horn	976
2. Trumpet	977
3. Flute or pipe	977
4. Double flute	977
5. Reeds or pan pipes	978
6. Bagpipe	978
III. Stringed instruments	978
1. Harp	978
2. Psaltery or dulcimer	978
Precious stones of the Bible	979
Ruby	981
Topaz	981
Garnet carbuncle	981
Emerald	981
Sapphire	981
Sardonyx	981
Diamond	981
White sapphire adamant	981
Jacinth	981
Agate	981
Amethyst	981
Beryl	981
Chalcedony	981
Onyx	982
Jasper	982
Carnelian	982
Chrysolite	982
Amber	982
Chrysoprase	982
Lapis lazuli	982
Pearl	982
A selection of the coins of Bible lands	982
Shekel	984
Two coins of John Hyrcanus	984
Widow's mite	984
Coin of Herod Antipas	984
Coin of Herod Philip II	985
Coin of Agrippa II	985
Denarius, or Roman tribute penny	985

EXHIBIT OF BIBLICAL ANTIQUITIES. 947

	Page.
A selection of the coins of Bible lands—Continued.	
Stater	985
Coin of Cæsarea	985
Tetradrachm of Sidon	986
Tetradrachms of Tyre	986
Coin of Ashkelon	986
Coins of the city of Damascus	986
Tetradrachm of the city of Babylon	986
Tetradrachm of Alexander the Great	986
Tetradrachm of Seleucus I, Nicator, King of Syria	986
Coin of Demetrius Soter	987
Stater of Tarsus	987
Coin of Cyprus	987
Tetradrachms of Ephesus	987
Hemidrachms of Ephesus	987
Aes (= As) of Thessalonica	987
Coin of Thessalonica	988
Tetradrachm of Macedonia	988
Didrachms of Athens	988
Tetradrachms of Athens	988
Child's bank	988
Dress, ornaments, and household utensils	988
Sheepskin coat	988
Male costume of Bagdad, Mesopotamia	989
Woman's costume of Bagdad, Mesopotamia	990
Syrian coat	990
Silver necklace	990
Silver anklets	990
Gold nose ring	990
Kohl and ancient and modern implements used in painting the eyes	991
Millstones	991
Goatskin waterbag	992
Bird trap	992
Sling	992
Wooden door lock and key	993
Syrian inkhorn	993
Jewish religious ceremonial	993
Manuscript copy of the Pentateuch, or five books of Moses in Hebrew	993
Pointer	993
Silver breastplate of the Torah	994
Veil of the Holy Ark	994
Sabbath lamp	994
Kiddush cloth	994
Silver spice box	995
Brass plate, used at the Passover meal	995
Omer tablet	995
Lulab and Ethrog	996
Manuscript copy of the Book of Esther	996
Lamp used at the feast of dedication	996
Knife and cup used at circumcision	997
Garment of fringes	997
Phylacteries	997
Silk prayer shawl	998
Gold wedding ring	998
Marriage contract	998
Mizrach	999

948   REPORT OF NATIONAL MUSEUM, 1896.

	Page.
Jewish religious ceremonial—Continued.	
Knife with its sheath	999
Antiquities	999
Egypt	999
Cast of a bust of Ramses II	999
Cast of a relief of Ramses II	1000
Cast of the head of Seti I	1001
Cast of a relief of Seti I	1001
Cast of the head of Tirhakah	1001
Mummy	1001
Model of a mummy	1003
Fragments of mummied dog, cat, crocodile, and other animals	1003
Book of the dead	1004
Two Scarabaei	1004
Egyptian brick	1004
Modern Egyptian brick from Thebes	1005
Egyptian cotton	1005
Assyria and Babylonia	1006
Cast of the so-called oval of Sargon	1006
Model of a temple tower of Babylon	1006
The Chaldean Deluge tablet	1007
Cast of a colossal human-headed winged lion	1008
Cast of the black Obelisk of Shalmaneser II	1008
Cast of a bell	1009
The Hittites	1010
Cast of a colossal statute of the god Hadad	1011
Hittite divinity	1012
Hittite winged divinity	1012
Hittite God of the Chase	1012
Hittite figure	1012
Hittite winged sphinx, with human head	1012
Hittite winged sphinx, with double head	1012
Hittite king	1012
Three Hittite warriors	1012
Hittite lute player	1013
Hittite lion chase	1013
Hittite warrior	1013
Collection of Bibles	1013
The Old Testament	1013
The New Testament	1014
Hebrew Bible, facsimile of Aleppo Codex	1014
Fragments of manuscript of the Hebrew Bible	1014
Printed editions of the Hebrew Bible	1015
Hebrew Bible without vowel points	1015
Hebrew Bible edited by Elias Hutter	1015
Hebrew Bible, first American edition	1015
Polychrome edition of the Old Testament	1016
Leicester Codex of the New Testament	1016
Greek and Latin New Testament of Erasmus	1016
Greek Testament, first American edition	1016
Greek Testament, second American edition	1016
Ancient versions of the Bible	1016
Targum or Aramean translation of the Old Testament	1017
Facsimile of manuscripts of the Septuagint	1017
Facsimile of the Codex Vaticanus	1017
Codex Sinaiticus	1017

Collection of Bibles—Continued.
    Ancient versions of the Bible—Continued.   Page.

	Page
Codex Alexandrinus	1018
The Vulgate or Latin Bible	1018
Syriac Old Testament	1018
Syriac New Testament	1018
Coptic New Testament	1019
Ethiopic version of the Bible	1019
Arabic version of Saadia Gaon	1019
Arabic Bible, manuscript	1019
Arabic New Testament	1019
Modern translations of the Bible	1019
The New Testament, translated by John Wycliffe	1019
Tyndale's New Testament	1019
The Gothic and Anglo-Saxon Gospels	1020
Coverdale's Bible	1020
The Genevan Version	1020
King James or Authorized Version	1020
The Revised Version	1021
Parallel New Testament	1021
The New Testament, translated by Tischendorf	1021
Luther's Bible	1021
Spanish Old Testament	1021
Eliot's Indian Bible	1022
Miniature Bible	1022
Cromwell's Soldier's Pocket Bible	1022
Hieroglyphic Bible	1023
Bishop Asbury's Testament	1023
Thomas Jefferson's Bible	1023

LIST OF ILLUSTRATIONS.

PLATES.

		Facing page.
1.	Musical instruments of percussion	974
2.	Wind musical instruments	976
3.	Trumpet. Morocco, Africa	978
4.	Assyrian bas-relief representing a flute player	978
5.	Arch of Titus at Rome, showing two trumpets from the Temple of Jerusalem	978
6.	Bagpipe. Tunis, Africa	978
7.	Assyrian bas-relief showing harp players	978
8.	Hittite lute player. Senjirli, Asia Minor	978
9.	Coins of Bible lands	982
10.	Sheepskin coat. Syria	988
11.	Eastern ornaments	990
12.	Millstones and goatskin waterbag	992
13.	Women grinding corn by hand mill	992
14.	Bird trap, sling, and door lock	992
15.	Breastplate of the Torah. Constantinople	994
16.	Veil of the Holy Ark (*Parocheth*). Constantinople	994
17.	Lamps and slaughtering knife. Germany	994
18.	Implements of circumcision, and spice-box	996
19.	Passover plate. Constantinople	996
20.	Omer tablet	996
21.	Phylacteries (*tefillin*)	998
22.	Marriage contract (*Kethubah*). Rome, Italy	998
23.	Mummy and cover of coffin. Luxor, Egypt	1002
24.	Mummy case	1002
25.	Model of a mummy and fragments of mummied animals. Egypt	1004
26.	Model of a Babylonian Temple Tower	1006
27.	Hadad. Gertchin, Northern Syria	1012
28.	Hittite Divinity with trident and hammer	1012
29.	Hittite Winged Divinity with head of Griffon. Senjirli, Asia Minor	1012
30.	Hittite God of the Chase holding hares. Senjirli, Asia Minor	1012
31.	Hittite figure surmounted by winged sun disk. Boghazkeui, Asia Minor	1012
32.	Hittite winged Sphinx with human head. Senjirli, Asia Minor	1012
33.	Hittite winged Sphinx with double head of man and lion. Senjirli, Asia Minor	1012
34.	Hittite King with scepter and spear. Senjirli, Asia Minor	1012
35.	Hittite warriors. Boghazkeui, Asia Minor	1012
36.	Hittite lion chase. Saktschegözu	1012
37.	Hittite warrior with ax and sword. Senjirli, Asia Minor	1012
38.	Facsimile of Aleppo Codex. Aleppo, Syria	1014
39.	Hebrew manuscript of the thirteenth century. Cairo, Egypt	1014
40.	Hebrew manuscript of the thirteenth century. Cairo, Egypt	1014
41.	First American edition of the Hebrew Bible	1016
42.	Greek and Latin New Testament of Erasmus	1016
43.	First American edition of the Greek New Testament	1016
44.	Arabic Bible. Cairo, Egypt	1018
45.	Title page of Eliot's Indian Bible	1022
46.	Hieroglyphic Bible	1024

BIBLICAL ANTIQUITIES.

A DESCRIPTION OF THE EXHIBIT AT THE COTTON STATES INTERNATIONAL EXPOSITION, ATLANTA, 1895.

By Cyrus Adler, Ph. D.,
Custodian, Section of Historic Religious Ceremonials, U. S. National Museum,
and
I. M. Casanowicz, Ph. D.
Aid, Division of Historic Archæology, U. S. National Museum.

INTRODUCTION.

The Section of Oriental Antiquities in the U. S. National Museum was established in 1887, and in 1889 there was added to the Museum a Section of Religious Ceremonial Institutions. Although not at all identical in scope, it was found best for practical reasons that the exhibit of these two sections in the Atlanta Exposition should be united in the form of a collection which, for want of a better name, may be called Biblical Antiquities. The space allowed was an alcove 20 by 20 feet. All of the subdivisions of this subject were represented, so that there was no possibility of completeness in any direction. Nevertheless, the exhibit had an educational value, as being the first collection put together at an exposition which attempted to show in outline all of the possibilities of study in this most important field.

It has, therefore, seemed proper that a record be made of this collection as it was actually shown at Atlanta, in the order in which it was shown, and without any attempt to fill out the deficiencies which are known to have existed. Such a description will, it is hoped, be of service to teachers and students, and may possibly furnish a suggestion to those who are interested in the establishment of small collections which touch the interests of so many persons, who, without being special students and investigators, are yet deeply concerned in anything that relates to the archæology and history, the ethnology, and the art of that portion of the eastern world around the Mediterranean, to which the culture and civilization of later Europe and even of modern America can in a great degree be traced.

The limitations of space caused some apparent incongruities; nevertheless, it can be said that nothing was shown which did not bear upon Biblical history and antiquities.

THE LAND OF THE BIBLE.

MAP OF PALESTINE.—It is not possible to understand the geology, the flora, and fauna of a country, the habits and customs of the people, nor their history, without an idea of the physical features of the country studied. The first object shown, therefore, was a relief map of Palestine. This map is the result of geographical and geological survey work, carried on for more than ten years by experts in the service of the Palestine Exploration Fund. It is 7 feet 9 inches by 4 feet 1 inch in size and made on the scale of $\frac{1}{168960}$, or three-eighths of an inch to the mile. It embraces the whole of western Palestine, from Baalbec in the north to Kadesh Barnea in the south, and shows nearly all that is known of the country east of the Jordan. The natural features of the country stand out prominently, being reinforced by appropriate colors. The mountains and plains are shaded a creamy white. The seas, lakes, marshes, and perennial streams are shown in blue. The Old and New Testament sites are marked in red. The map thus furnishes a most important aid for the understanding of the Bible narrative.[1]

GEOLOGY.

No attempt was made to present in systematic form the geology of the country nor to show in any way the features of the soil. The following specimens, which possess a sentimental interest merely, were placed in the collection.

DUST FROM JERUSALEM.—Dust from the Holy Land is with many Jews a much-cherished possession, perhaps suggested by Psalms cii, 14: "For thy servants take pleasure in her stones, and have pity upon her dust." It is sometimes placed in the graves, and is considered as a substitute for actual burial in the Holy Land, which is one of the pious aspirations of the orthodox Jew.

WATER FROM THE JORDAN.—The Jordan is one of the points of attraction for pilgrims to Palestine. As early as the time of Constantine (306 to 337) baptism in the Jordan was deemed a special privilege, on account of its association with John the Baptist and the baptism of Christ;[2] even now the Oriental Christians attach great importance to the bath in the Jordan, as the termination of a pilgrimage.[3]

The pilgrims usually fill jars from the river to be used for baptisms at home.

SMALL SHELL (*Janthina fragilis*) FROM TYRE.—Tyre was in ancient times the wealthiest and most magnificent of Phenician cities. It was situated on the Mediterranean, and consisted of two parts, Palaetyrus on the mainland and Neotyrus on the island. It was famous for the

---

[1] Compare the Survey of Western Palestine; the Survey of Eastern Palestine, and the Geology of Palestine and Arabia Petræa, published by the Palestine Exploration Fund.

[2] Matthew iii, 13–17.

[3] For a description of the bathing of the pilgrims see Sinai and Palestine, by Dean Stanley, New York, 1883, pp. 384–386.

precious purple dye, which was extensively prepared from the shellfish Murex. Tyre is often mentioned in the Bible under the name of Çor.[1] The modern Çur, on its site, is an unimportant town of about 5,000 inhabitants.

GRANITE FROM JEBEL MUSA.—Jebel Musa (mountain of Moses) is one of the peaks in the southeast of the Sinaitic Mountain range. It rises about 7,000 feet above the sea level, and tradition assigns to it the giving of the Law to Moses. The Sinaitic Mountain chain is formed of granite and porphyry. The quarries and mineral deposits of the Sinaitic Peninsula were worked as early as 3,000 B. C.

FLORA.

The flora, like the geology of the country, was but inadequately represented, the following specimens being the only ones shown:

SEED PODS OF THE CAROB TREE.—The carob or locust tree (*Ceratonia siliqua*) is common in Galilee, in the plain of Sharon, and in the countries around the Mediterranean Sea in general. The island of Cyprus alone produces at present about 30,000 tons of carobs, almost the whole of which is exported to England and France, and "this quantity is produced by hardly a third of the carob trees growing in the island, because perhaps the other two-thirds of these trees are not yet grafted."[2] Its fruit is a brown pod, from 6 to 12 inches long, about an inch broad, having a fleshy or mealy pulp, of an agreeable taste, which is not only ground up for cattle and swine, but also extensively used as food by the Arabs, Moors, and Italians. Large quantities of carob are used, especially in France, for distillation, and also for producing a sort of molasses[3] The English name is borrowed from the Oriental, probably coming from the Arabic[4] *Harrûb* through Spanish; it occurs in the Talmud in the form *Harûb*. It is generally assumed that the carob beans represent the "husks," in the Revised Version "pods of the carob tree," (in the Greek original κεράτιον, *keration*) in the parable of the Prodigal Son.[5] Through a confusion between the pods of the carob tree (also called locust) with the locusts (insects, Greek ἀκρίδες, *akrides*) which John the Baptist ate,[6] it was thought that the pods formed the food of John the Baptist, and they are still commonly called "St. John's bread."

SYCAMORE FROM PALESTINE.—The sycamore tree (*Ficus sycomorus*), Hebrew *shiqmah*, is represented in I Kings x, 27, as having been abundant in Palestine in the reign of Solomon: "The king made silver to be in Jerusalem as stones, and cedars made he to be as the sycamore trees that are in the lowland for abundance," and similarly we read in

---

[1] Ezekiel xxvi–xxviii, etc.
[2] P. G. Gennadius, Report on the Agriculture of Cyprus, Pt. 1, p. 17.
[3] *Idem.*, pp. 18, 19.
[4] It also occurs in French. See Remarques sur les mots français dérivés de l'arabe, par Henri Sommens, S. J., Beyrouth, 1890, p. 18.
[5] Luke xv, 16.
[6] Matthew iii, 4.

Isaiah ix, 9, 10, "the sycamores are cut down, but we will change them into cedars." The sycamore of the Bible has no natural alliance with the maple sycamores of Europe and North America. In flowers and foliage it closely resembles the common fig, but grows to a greater size, sometimes reaching a height of 30 or 40 feet and a diameter of 20 feet. It bears at least two crops annually, but they are small and insipid compared with those of the common fig tree (*Ficus carica*). Still they are gathered and used as food by the poorer classes. The prophet Amos describes himself as a "dresser of sycamore trees."[1] In the Egyptian cult the sycamore was symbolical of the tree of life, being dedicated to Hathor.

APPLES OF SODOM.—The apples of Sodom are considered by some to represent the nightshade (*Solanum sanctum*) which grows in bushes and thickets in warm regions and especially in the Jordan Valley. It is a shrubby plant, 3 or 4 feet high. Its blossoms resemble in color and form those of the potato, and the fruits are oval-shaped, first of yellow, but when ripe of a beautiful red color. The fruit is said to be turned into dust by the sting of an insect, leaving only the skin intact. Robinson identifies the fruit of the *Asclepias gigantea* with the apples of Sodom. This fruit resembles a large yellow apple. Externally of fair appearance, it bursts when pressed like a bubble filled with air, leaving only the shreds of a thin skin in the hand. The Orientals describe the *Asclepias gigantea* as a plant containing an astringent milky juice. (Arabic, *Yatū*. Syriac, *Yetūa sebe'a helba*.[2])

UNRIPE POMEGRANATE FROM PALESTINE.—The pomegranate (*Punica granatum;* Hebrew, *Rimmón*) is enumerated among the plants characteristic of the promised land,[3] though it was not native there; it was and continues to be extensively cultivated in Palestine, and its failure is represented as a special punishment of God.[4] It grows wild in Persia, Afghanistan, and neighboring countries, and has been cultivated from time immemorial along the north and south coasts of the Mediterranean.[5]

It is still common in Tunis and Algiers, where it is called by the Arabs *rimán*, corresponding exactly to the ancient Hebrew name. It is a beautiful shrub, with dark and shining leaves and bell-shaped flowers. In the autumn it yields a ruddy fruit about the size of an orange, usually of a reddish tint, filled with a delicious pulp, in which semitransparent seeds lie in rows. It was appreciated for its fruit[6] and its wine,[7] which is made from the fermented juice. Its fruits and flowers were also used in medicine, and the rind for tanning leather. The manufacture of leather by means of it was introduced by the

---

[1] Amos vii, 14.
[2] Immanuel Loew, Aramaeische Pflanzennamen, Leipzig, 1881, p. 192.
[3] Deuteronomy viii, 8: "A land of pomegranates."
[4] Joel i, 12.
[5] Pliny Nat. Hist., XIII, 34.
[6] Canticles iv, 13: "an orchard of pomegranates with precious fruits."
[7] *Idem* viii, 2.

Moors from Africa into Spain, especially into Cordova, and the leather was hence called "Cordovan." It is still used in Morocco, the leather of which country retains its superiority, especially for bookbinding. The flowers and fruit of the pomegranate entered into the religious rites and symbolism of the Phenicians and ancient Romans, as well as of the ancient Israelites. The robe of the High Priest had an embroidery of "pomegranates of blue and of purple and of scarlet round about the skirt thereof,"[1] while the pomegranate also formed a decorative symbol in the columns of the Temple.[2] Hehn[3] says: "Religious intercourse in ancient times also brought the glorious pomegranate tree to Europe. Its purple blossoms in brilliant foliage and red-cheeked fruit rich in kernels must have from the beginning excited the imagination of the peoples of Western Asia, whose mode of thinking was symbolical. In the Odyssey, among the fruits in the garden of the king of the Pheaks, and among those that torment by their sight, the Phrygian Tantalus are also the pomegranates $ῥοισί$ (rhoisi), which name in itself bears decisive testimony to the origin of the plant in Semitic language and culture." "The name of the pomgranate fruit among the Portuguese is to the present day the Arabic roma, romeira."[4]

CONE OF THE CEDAR OF LEBANON.—The cedar of Lebanon (Cedrus libani, Hebrew Erez) has its chief habitat in the ranges of the Taurus and Lebanon, the latter being its southernmost limit. The Old Testament abounds in references to the cedar of Lebanon. It was considered as the prince of trees, the emblem of all that is grand, magnificent, and durable: "The glory of Lebanon;[5] the trees of the Lord are satisfied; the cedars of Lebanon, which He hath planted;"[6] "the righteous shall flourish like the palm tree; he shall grow like a cedar in Lebanon."[7] Frequent references are also made to the economic uses of the cedar. It supplied the chief material for the woodwork of the temple of Solomon and the royal palaces,[8] the second temple of Zerubbabel,[9] and according to Josephus[10] was also used in the rebuilding of the temple by Herod. From the Assyrian inscriptions it is learned that the Assyrian kings procured the costly woods for their buildings from the Lebanon. Cedar timber was also used in the great Persian edifices at Persepolis, in the first temple of Diana at Ephesus, and that of Apollo at Utica, where the age of the cedar timber was computed at two thousand years. At present the forest of Lebanon

---

[1] Exodus xxviii, 33, 34.

[2] I Kings vii, 18-20.

[3] Kulturpflanzen und Hausthiere in ihrem Übergang aus Asien nach Griechenland und Italien sowie in das übrige Europa. Historisch-linguistische Skizzen, Berlin, 1870, p. 155.

[4] Quoted by Loew, p. 362.

[5] Isaiah xxxv, 2.

[6] Psalms civ, 16.

[7] Idem xcii, 12.

[8] I Kings vi and vii.

[9] Ezra iii, 7.

[10] Jewish War, v, 5, 2.

"is shorn of its glory," and only between 400 and 500 cedar trees are found in small groups in various parts of the mountain range, most of them in the valley of Kadisha, nearly 7,000 feet above the sea. The tree is still called by the Arabs *Arz*, identical with the ancient Hebrew name.[1]

CONE OF A LEBANON FIR.—The Hebrew word[2] *Berosh*, which is rendered by the English version "fir," probably comprises the other coniferous trees of Palestine, including junipers, pines, and the funeral cypress. Of the pine there are four species in Palestine. The most common is the Aleppo pine (*Pinus halepensis*), then the pinaster (*P. pinaster*), the stone (*P. pinea*), and the Pyrenean (*P. pyrenaica*). The *Juniperus excelsa* is very common, and the *Cypressus sempervirens* is the common species of western Asia and southern Europe. "Fir trees" are frequently referred to in the Old Testament in association with cedars of Lebanon, though the former were deemed inferior: "Howl, O fir tree, for the cedar is fallen."[3] "Fir" timber was used for the floors of the temple,[4] for ships' planks,[5] and for musical instruments.[6] The fruit is but once mentioned: "I am like a green fir tree; from me is thy fruit found."[7]

FAUNA.

Though for obvious reasons no attempt was made at a compete collection of the fauna of the Bible, a sufficient number of specimens was shown from each class to make the exhibit of this division of the natural history of the Bible in some measure representative.

MAMMALS.

The mammals were illustrated by the following specimens:

THE APE[8] (*Hanuman monkey, Semnopithecus entellus*; Hebrew, *Qof*).—The ape was not native in Palestine. It is mentioned in the Bible among the commodities brought to Solomon by the ships of Tarshish.[9] The Hebrew name for ape is cognate with that in the Tamil language (*Kapi*), and it is therefore assumed that the apes were brought from Ceylon or South India, where the genus *Semnopithecus* is especially frequent. The ape has also been identified among the animals depicted on the Assyrian monuments.

THE BAT (Hebrew, *Atallef*).—The bat is classed in the catalogue of animals[10] among the unclean birds, which are forbidden for food. In

---

[1] Immanuel Loew, Aramaeische Pflanzennamen, Leipzig, 1881, p. 57.
[2] Some authorities favor the rendering cypress.
[3] Zachariah xi. 2.
[4] I Kings vi, 15. The Revised Version gives cypress in the margin.
[5] Ezekiel xxvii, 5.
[6] II Samuel vi, 5.
[7] Hosea xiv, 8.
[8] Since the version of 1611 English usage has changed. Monkey, the more general term, would be a fitter rendering.
[9] I Kings x, 22, and the parallel passages in II Chronicles ix, 21.
[10] Leviticus xi, 19, 20; compare Deuteronomy xiv, 18.

Isaiah ii, 20, 21, bats are alluded to in company with moles as inhabiting holes and cavities about ruins; "In that day a man shall cast away his idols of silver, and his idols of gold which they made for him to worship, to the moles and to the bats to go into the caverns of the rocks, and into the clefts of the ragged rocks." Bats are still very numerous in Palestine, about twenty species being known. One of the most common is *Cynonycteris ægyptiaca*, a specimen of which was shown.

"CONEY" ROCK-BADGER (*Procavia syriaca*, or *Hyrax syriacus*; Hebrew, *Shafan*).—In the English versions of the Bible the Hebrew *Shafan* is rendered "coney," which formerly was the common name for rabbit, although that usage is now obsolete. It is well known that the introduction of the rabbit into the East is of recent date, and that no rabbit was known to the ancient inhabitants of Bible lands.[1] Besides, while the rabbit has its dwelling place in sand or clay, the *Shafan* is enumerated in the Bible[2] among the "four things little upon earth, but exceeding wise, being but a feeble folk, yet they make their houses in the rock," and their attachment to rocks is also referred to in Psalms civ, 18: "The rocks are refuge for the *shefanim*." The animal mentioned in these passages can not, therefore, have been a rabbit, and it is now assumed by all writers to be the *Procavia* or *Hyrax syriacus*, which belongs to an isolated group of hoofed mammals whose dentition manifests considerable similarity to the teeth of the rhinoceros. The hyrax is not as common in Palestine as formerly, but it is still found in some places, as in the gorge of the Kedron, on the west side of the Dead Sea, while at the summit of Jebel Musa, on Mount Sinai, a whole colony is in existence. The Arabs call the hyrax *wabr*, and describe it as the "little animal of the children of Israel" (*janamu bani Israil*).[3] In Abyssinia the hyrax is called *gehejat*, and its flesh is there used as food by the Mohammedans.[4] The Israelites counted it among the unclean animals.[5]

YOUNG CAMEL (*Camelus dromedarius*, Hebrew *Gamal*).—The camel was, and is still, one of the most useful beasts in Palestine. It is referred to in the Bible as being used for riding,[6] as a beast of burden,[7] and of draft.[8] It was also used in war.[9] Among Jacob's gifts to Esau were thirty milch camels (literally, "camels giving suck") with their colts.[10] The flesh of the camel was forbidden as food.[11] It is eaten now when better food can not be had in most parts of the East; but the meat is

---

[1] W. Houghton, Gleanings from the Natural History of the Ancients, pp. 139, 181.
[2] Proverbs xxx, 24 and 26.
[3] Fritz Hommel, Die Namen der Säugethiere bei den Südsemitischen Völkern, p. 322.
[4] Dr. B. Longravel in Zoologische Jahrbuecher, III, p. 336.
[5] Leviticus xi, 5; Deuteronomy xiv, 7.
[6] Genesis xxiv, 64.
[7] *Idem* xxxvii, 25; I Kings x, 2, etc.
[8] Isaiah xxi, 7.
[9] I Samuel xxx, 17.
[10] Genesis xxxii, 15.
[11] Leviticus xi, 4; Deuteronomy xiv, 7.

said to be very coarse and dry. The meat of a very young camel, however, is esteemed by the Arabs as a great luxury. The camel had many uses in the arts. Camel's hair was used for weaving into cloth. John the Baptist "had his raiment of camel's hair."[1] Tents, shields, harness, saddles, and even trunks are made of camel's skin. Two species, the one-humped camel (*Camelus dromedarius*) and the Bactrian two-humped camel (*Camelus bactrianus*), were known in Palestine, the former being more frequent. The camel was the subject of many proverbial expressions, two of which are by Jesus, Matthew xix, 24: "It is easier for a camel to go through a needle's eye than for a rich man to enter into the Kingdom of God," and xxiii, 24: "Strain out the gnat and swallow the camel." The word for camel is practically the same in most ancient and modern languages.

GAZELLE (*Gazella dorcas*; Hebrew, *Çebi*).—The gazelle (in the Authorized Version "roebuck," also translated "roe" in the Revised Version) was allowed as food.[2] It was provided for the royal table of Solomon.[3] The characteristics of swiftness and gentleness of these animals are often referred to[4] "as light of foot as a wild roe;"[5] "as swift as the roes upon the mountains;"[6] "The voice of my beloved; behold he cometh leaping upon the mountains, skipping upon the hills. My beloved is like a roe or a young hart."[7] The feminine form, in Hebrew *Çebiah*, in Aramean *Tabitha*, was often used as a proper name;[8] for example, "Now there was at Joppa a certain disciple named Tabitha, which by interpretation is called Dorcas." The Arabs call the gazelle *tabi* and employ it frequently in their love poetry as the image of feminine loveliness. More than twenty species of gazelle inhabit Africa, Arabia, Persia, India, and central Asia. The gazelle of Syria, Egypt, and Arabia is the *Gazella dorcas*. It is very common in Palestine, especially in the Judean wilderness and the Arabah.

MOUSE (Hebrew, *Akbar*).—The mouse is enumerated among the unclean "creeping things,"[9] "eating swine's flesh, and the abomination, and the mouse." Mice were sent as a plague upon the Philistines for having carried off the Ark of the Covenant.[10] No less than twenty species have been found in Palestine. The *Mus bactrianus*, which is especially plentiful and familiar, was given as an illustration.

BIRDS.

The birds enumerated in the Bible were represented by fourteen specimens.

THE COCK.—No mention is made of the cock in the Old Testament, but in the New Testament he is referred to in connection with Peter's

---

[1] Matthew iii, 4; Mark i, 6.
[2] Deuteronomy xii, 15, 22; xiv, 5; xv, 22.
[3] I Kings iv, 23.
[4] II Samuel ii, 18.
[5] I Chronicles xii, 8.
[6] Canticles ii, 8.
[7] *Idem*, viii, 14.
[8] II Kings xii; I Acts ix, 36.
[9] Leviticus xi, 29; Isaiah lxvi, 17.
[10] I Samuel vi.

denial of Jesus, when Jesus said to Peter, "The cock shall not crow this day until thou shalt thrice deny that thou knowest me."[1] It is said that in remembrance of the crowing of the cock, which brought Peter to a sense of his guilt, the practice began of placing weathercocks upon towers and steeples.[2]

There is independent testimony from the Mishna that the cock had become common in Palestine. The Mishna was collected about 200 of the Christian era, but as many portions of it go back to at least three centuries earlier it is in some portions contemporary with and even earlier than the New Testament. According to the Mishna[3] the Jews were prohibited from selling a white cock to the heathens. This prohibition was compromised by the permission to sell if the toe were cut off, because "they do not sacrifice anything defective." The word for cock is "*Tarnegol*," Syriac *Tarnagla*. There is no Biblical Hebrew word for cock. In addition to the above the Talmud uses the word *Geber*, which means simply "male." The crowing of the cock is referred to a number of times in the Talmud, cock crow being a recognized time.[4] There are three that are strong (unyielding), says the Talmud, "Israel among the peoples; the dog among the beasts, and the cock among the birds." (*Beça* 5b.)

On Babylonian gems the cock appears as the herald of dawn, the heavenly guardian of light, who by his crowing drives away the demons of the night. The native country of the domestic cock is supposed to be India, and the migration of domestic fowl to western Asia and Europe probably took place with the Medo-Persian conquerors. As the Persians spread their dominions, the cock, the "Persian bird" went with them.

TURTLEDOVE (*Turtur risorius*; Hebrew, *Tor*).—The turtledove and the dove or pigeon (Hebrew, *Yonah*) are very frequently mentioned in the Bible. They were the only birds permitted as sacrifices.[5] Noah sent forth a dove three times from the ark. On its second flight it returned with an olive leaf,[6] which has since been regarded as the emblem of peace. Numerous allusions are made in the Scriptures to the simplicity, innocence, gentleness, and fidelity of the dove:[7] "Ephraim is like a silly dove without understanding."[8] "Be ye therefore wise as serpents, and harmless as doves." The turtledove is noted for the regularity of its migration:[9] "And the turtle and the swallow and the crane observe the time of their coming," compare Canticles ii, 11, 12. At present there are four species of dove and three species of turtledove inhabiting Palestine in large numbers.

GOLDEN EAGLE (*Aquila chrysaëtos*; Hebrew, *Nesher*).—The Hebrew

---

[1] Luke xxii, 34; John xiii, 38.
[2] Layard, Nineveh and Babylon, p. 458.
[3] Aboda Zara Idolatry, I, 5.
[4] Mishna Yoma, I, 8.
[5] Leviticus i, 14; v, 7; xii, 8; Luke ii, 24.
[6] Genesis viii, 8–11.
[7] Hosea vii, 11.
[8] Matthew x, 16.
[9] Jeremiah viii, 7.

term *Nesher*, which in the English Bible is invariably rendered "eagle," comprises large birds of prey in general, and perhaps particularly the griffon vulture. The golden eagle is quite common in Palestine. At least seven other distinct kinds have been observed. Numerous references are found in the Bible to the characteristics of the eagle: Its high soaring in the air;[1] its molting, as a symbol of the renewing of strength;[2] its strength;[3] its predatory habits;[4] its power of vision;[5] its care for its young, in comparison with God's sheltering care over his people.[6] The eagle, as emblematic of the divine attributes, is one of the four living creatures in the vision of Ezekiel (i, 10) and in the Apocalypse of John (iv, 7). It is also the emblem of John the Evangelist.

HOOPOE (*Upupa epops*; Hebrew, *Dukifath*).—It is probable that the Hebrew name *dukifath*, occurring in the list of unclean birds,[7] denotes the hoopoe, as the Revised Version translates it, and not the "lapwing," as rendered by the Authorized Version. The hoopoe feeds on insects in dunghills and marshy places, and is therefore considered a very filthy bird. It is very common in Egypt, where it is found throughout the winter. In Palestine it is a summer visitor. The Egyptians considered the hoopoe as symbolical of gratitude, because it repays the early kindness of its parents in their old age by trimming their wings and bringing them food when they are acquiring new plumage. The Arabs call it the "doctor," believing it to possess marvelous medicinal qualities, and they use its head in charms and incantations.

OWL.—Various Hebrew names are assigned by the English Version to different species of owl—*Yanshuf*, Leviticus xi, 17; Deuteronomy xiv, 16, "great owl;" *Kos*, in the same passage, "little owl.[8]

The owl belonged to the unclean birds, and is enumerated among the animals inhabiting deserted and dismal places.[9] The Egyptian eagle owl (*Bubo ascalaphus*) and the little owl (*Athene glaux*) are the most common species in Palestine. The latter known by the name of *Boomeh*

---

[1] Isaiah xl, 31: "They shall mount up with wings as eagles." Jeremiah xlix, 16, etc.

[2] "Thy youth is renewed like the eagle."—Psalms ciii, 5.

[3] Hosea viii, 1: "As an eagle he cometh against the house of the Lord."

[4] Job ix, 26: "As the eagle that swoopeth on the prey. Compare Proverbs xxx, 17; Matthew xxiv, 28.

[5] Job xxxix, 28, 29: "She dwelleth on the rock, and hath her lodging there upon the crag of the rock and the strong hold. From thence she spieth out the prey; her eyes behold it afar off."

[6] Deuteronomy xxxii, 11: "As an eagle that stirreth up her nest, that fluttereth over her young, he spread abroad his wings, he took them, he bare them on his pinions."

[7] Deuteronomy xiv, 18; Leviticus xi, 19.

[8] These names are disputed; some translate *Yanshuf* by "water fowl;" *Kos* by pelican, or falcon. Lilith (Isaiah xxxiv, 14), which is rendered in the Authorized Version by screech owl, in all probability means simply a specter. It is rendered in the Revised Version "night monster."

[9] Psalms cii, 6: "I am become as an owl of the waste places."

among the Arabs, is also called the "mother of ruins," as no ruin or tomb of pretension will readily be found without one. This species is a great favorite with the Arabs, being regarded as lucky and friendly to man.

PARTRIDGE (*Caccabis chucar*, Hebrew *Qore*).—Reference is made to the partridge in Samuel xxvi, 20, "as when one doth hunt a partridge in the mountains," and in Jeremiah xvii, 11, as the partridge (margin of Revised Version "sitteth on eggs which she hath not laid,") "gathereth young which she hath not brought forth," alluding to the ancient belief that the partridge was in the habit of stealing eggs and hatching them. Besides the chucar partridge, Hey's sand partridge (*Ammoperdix heyi*) is abundant in Palestine and in Sinai.

PEACOCK (*Pavo cristatus*; Hebrew, *Tukkiyim*).—The peacock is mentioned among the animals brought by Solomon's ships from Tarshish.[1] It is an Indian bird, and the Hebrew name can be traced to the Tamil *tokei* Malabar *tógai, tóghai*, "the crested bird." In some parts of India it is very abundant and almost domesticated. It is venerated by the Hindus, and large flocks are kept at their temples. It made its appearance in Greece in the middle of the fifth century B. C., and was adopted at Samos as the sacred bird of Hera (Juno) at the temple of that goddess, the Heræum.

PELICAN (*Pelecanus onocrotalus*; Hebrew, *Qa'ath*).—The pelican is one of the unclean birds,[2] being regarded as an emblem of desolation and ruin.[3] From the habit of this bird of storing quantities of food in the large pouch attached to its lower mandible, for the purpose of feeding its young, which it does by pressing its beak against its breast, the fable arose that the pelican opened its breast with its beak and fed its young with its own blood, which seemed to derive support from the red tips at the end of the bill. Besides the common white pelican another species, the Dalmatian pelican (*Pelecanus crispus*), is found, but less commonly, on the coast of Syria.

QUAIL (*Coturnix communis*; Hebrew, *Selav*).—Quails are mentioned in the Bible only in connection with the miraculous supply of food which they formed for the Israelites upon two occasions, in the wilderness of Sin[4] and at Kibroth Hataavah.[5] They are the smallest representatives of the partridge family and breed in numbers in Palestine. They arrive in vast flocks by night in March and a few remain throughout the winter. Their flesh is considered a delicacy.

RAVEN (*Corvus corax*; Hebrew, *Oreb*).—The raven is the first bird mentioned by name in the Bible:[6] "And he sent forth a raven, and it

---
[1] I Kings x, 22; II Chronicles ix, 21.
[2] Leviticus xi, 18; Deuteronomy xiv, 17.
[3] Isaiah xxxiv, 11: "But the pelican and porcupine shall possess it;" Zephaniah ii, 14: "Both the pelican and the porcupine shall lodge in the chapters thereof."
[4] Exodus xvi, 13.
[5] Numbers xi, 31–32; compare Psalms lxxviii, 27, and cv, 40.
[6] Genesis viii, 7.

went forth to and fro, until the waters were dried up from off the earth." It was forbidden for food.[1] In several passages the raven is referred to as illustrating the care with which God watches over his creatures.[2] "He giveth to the beast his food, and to the young ravens which cry."[3] "Who provideth for the raven his food, when his young ones cry unto God, and wander for lack of meat."[4] "Consider the ravens, that they sow not, neither reap; which have no store chamber nor barn; and God feedeth them; of how much more value are ye than the birds." The custom of the ravens of attacking the eyes of young or sickly animals is alluded to in Proverbs xxx, 17: "The eye that mocketh at his father and despiseth to obey his mother, the ravens of the valley shall pick it out, and the young eagles shall eat it." The raven and allied species are abundant in Palestine.

SPARROW (*Passer domesticus*; Hebrew, *Çippor*).—The Hebrew word *çippor* denotes birds in general, being used especially, however, of small birds. In the following passages it appears to refer to the sparrow in particular: Psalm lxxxiv, 3: "The sparrow hath found her an house, and the swallow a nest for herself, where she may lay her young;" and Psalms cii, 7: "I watch, and become like a sparrow that is alone upon the house top." Jesus refers to the sparrow in illustration of God's benignant care of his creatures:[5] "Are not two sparrows sold for a farthing? and not one of them shall fall to the ground without your Father. But the very hairs of your head are all numbered. Fear not therefore, ye are of more value than many sparrows."[6] Several species of the sparrow occur in great abundance in Palestine, especially on the Plain of Gennesareth.

BLACK STORK (*Ciconia nigra*; Hebrew, *Hasidah*).—The stork was accounted an unclean bird.[7] It is a migrant,[8] "Yea, the stork in the heavens knoweth her appointed times," and built its nest in "the fir trees."[9] The Hebrew name *Hasidah* means the kind, the pious one (Latin, *pia avis*), owing to the filial piety and devotion which was attributed by the ancients to this bird.

The passage in Job xxxix, 13: "The wing of the ostrich rejoiceth, but her pinions and feathers are kindly (Hebrew, *hasidah*)" is thought to contain an allusion to the stork, whose treatment of the young is so different from that of the hard-breasted ostrich.[10]

Owing to this belief and to its feeding on noxious reptiles and insects

---

[1] Leviticus xi, 15; Deuteronomy xiv, 14.
[2] Psalms cxlvii, 9.
[3] Job xxxviii, 41.
[4] Luke xii, 24.
[5] Matthew x, 29-31.
[6] See also Luke xii, 6, 7.
[7] Leviticus xi, 19; Deuteronomy xiv, 18.
[8] Jeremiah viii, 7.
[9] Psalms civ, 17.
[10] I. M. Casanowicz Paronomasia in the Old Testament, p. 57.

the stork is a protected bird, and in parts of Europe and the East there is a heavy fine for molesting either the storks or their nests. Both the black and the white stork (*Ciconia alba*) occur in Palestine, the latter chiefly in winter; the former a migrant, passing to the north.

SWALLOW (*Chelidon rustica;* Hebrew, *Sis, Sus,* and *Deror*).—The swallow is referred to in Jeremiah viii, 7, as one of the birds which "observe the time of their coming." "As the sparrow in her wandering, as the swallow in her flying, so the curse that is causeless lighteth not."[1] Psalms, lxxxiv, 3: "Yea, the sparrow hath found her an house and the swallow a nest for herself." There are about half a dozen species of the swallow, and the closely allied martin, in Palestine. The common swallow abounds in the Mosque of Omar.

GRIFFON VULTURE (*Gyps fulvus*).—As was stated above under eagle, the Hebrew *Nesher*, which is rendered in the English Bible "eagle" comprises large predatory birds in general. Thus in Jeremiah xlix, 16, and Job xxxix, 27-30, the "eagle" is referred to as making its nest in the highest cliffs. "O, thou that dwellest in the clefts of the rock, that holdest the height of the hill; though thou shouldest make thy nest as high as the eagle, I will bring thee down from thence, saith the Lord": "Doth the eagle mount up at thy command, and make her nest on high? She dwelleth on the rock, and hath her lodging there, upon the crag of the rock, and the strong hold." This is especially characteristic of the griffon vulture. The passage in Micah i, 16; "Make thee bald * * * enlarge thy baldness as the eagle" can only refer to the vulture, which is devoid of true feathers on the head and neck. The griffon vulture is most abundant in Palestine. It breeds in colonies of aeries, the most notable of which are at Wady Kelt near Jericho, Mount Nebo, in the gorges of the Jabbok and the Litany River, at Mount Carmel, and in the valleys leading into the Plain of Genessareth.

REPTILES.

But four specimens of the reptiles of the Bible were exhibited.

FROG (Hebrew, *Çefarde'a*).—The frog is only mentioned in the Old Testament as the second plague inflicted on Egypt.[2] In Revelations xvi, 13, unclean spirits are spoken of as being in the likeness of frogs, which come out of the mouth of the dragon. The edible frog (*Rana esculenta*) is the only species which at present occurs in Egypt. In Palestine are found the green toad (*Bufo viridis*), and less commonly the African toad (*Bufo regularis*). The little tree frog (*Hyla arborea*) is also common in Sinai and Palestine.

LIZARD.—Leviticus xi, 30, mentions the names of a number of animals which are included among the creeping things that creep upon the earth. The *Leta'ah* (*Lacerta viridis* and *L. agilis*) is the only one traditionally rendered by lizard; but the present opinion is that the other names

---

[1] Proverbs xxvi, 2; compare Isaiah xxxviii, 14.
[2] Exodus viii, 2-14; compare Psalms lxxvii, 45; cv, 30.

are also kinds of lizards—the Revised Version furnishes this statement in the margin and translates great lizard, lizard, sand lizard, etc. The best lexicographical authority agrees with this view. Nor are we to be surprised at this number of words in Hebrew for lizard, since they are very abundant in Palestine, about forty species having been enumerated. Among the most common is the green lizard and its varieties.

VIPER (*Vipera aspis;* Hebrew, *Ef'eh*).—The generic name in Hebrew of any serpent is *Nahash*. The serpent is first mentioned in Genesis iii, 1, 13, where it is said to be more subtle than all the beasts of the field. Jesus alludes to the wisdom of the serpent,[1] "Be ye therefore wise as serpents and harmless as doves." The different species are referred to by various names—*pethen, shefifon, 'akshub,* and *çif'oni,* usually rendered by adder. The viper is mentioned in Isaiah xxx, 6; lix, 5; Job xx, 16: "The viper's tongue shall slay him," and often in the New Testament.[2] It is assumed that the viper that fastened on the hand of the Apostle Paul[3] was the *Vipera aspis*. Upward of thirty species have been found in Palestine.

INSECTS.

Six specimens of the insects of the Bible concluded the illustration of the Biblical fauna.

HORSEFLY (*Hippobosca equina;* Hebrew, *Arob*).—It is probable that the horsefly is meant by *arob* (English versions, "swarms of flies," "divers sorts of flies"), sent as a plague upon Egypt.[4] The rendering, "swarms of flies," as indicating a mixture of various insects, is very old, being found in the Talmud and in Jerome. The horsefly in Egypt settles on the human body, sucks blood, and produces festering sores. It is also the means of spreading ophthalmia.

BREEZE FLIES (*Hæmatopota pluvialis* and *Chrysops-coecutiens,* Hebrew *Zebub*).—The name *Zebub* occurs but twice in the Old Testament, Isaiah vii, 18, as a figure of swarming and troublesome armies coming from Egypt, "The Lord shall hiss for the fly that is in the uttermost part of the rivers of Egypt and for the bee that is in the land of Assyria;" and Ecclesiastes x, 1, as corrupting ointment, "Dead flies cause the ointment of the perfumer to send forth a stinking savor; so doth a little folly outweigh wisdom and honor." A species of *Tabanus* or breeze fly is common in the valleys of the Jordan and the Nile, and is very injurious to animals; it attacks both man and beast.[5]

The Phenicians invoked against the flies Baalzebub,[6] the lord of flies, the god of Ekron.[7]

---

[1] Matthew x, 16.
[2] Matthew iii, 7.
[3] Acts xxviii, 3.
[4] Exodus vii, 21-31; compare Psalms lxxviii, 45; cv, 31.
[5] Hart, Animals of the Bible, p. 101, 102; compare also Smith Dictionary, see *Baal*.
[6] In the New Testament, Beelzebub, Matthew x, 25.
[7] II Kings i, 2.

SACRED SCARABAEUS (*Ateuchus sacer*).—The *Ateuchus* was worshiped by the ancient Egyptians, and often represented by hieroglyphics and on monuments. Models of them in the most precious materials were worn as charms and buried with mummies. The insects themselves have also been found in coffins. It may be that the worship of the scarabaeus in Egypt was in some way connected with that of Baalzebub, the lord of flies, in Ekron.[1]

HORNET (*Vespa orientalis;* Hebrew, *Çir'ah*).—Hornets are spoken of in the Bible as an instrument in God's hands for the punishment and expulsion of the Canaanites.[2] "I will send the hornet before thee, which shall drive out the Hivite, the Canaanite, and the Hittite from before thee."[3] It is assumed by some that they are used figuratively for panic or terror. Hornets are abundant in Palestine, and were so in former times, as is perhaps indicated from the name of the city in Judah, Çore'ah, "place of hornets." There are at present four species in Palestine; the most common is *Vespa orientalis*.

LOCUST (*Acridium peregrinum;* Hebrew, *Arbeh*).—Of all the "creeping creatures" the locust is most frequently mentioned in the Bible. It occurs under nine different names (*hagab, hargol, sol'am, gazam, yeleq, hasil, geb or gob, çelaçal*), which probably denote different species. Locusts were one of the ten plagues inflicted on Egypt.[4] They were permitted as food,[5] and were the chief food of John the Baptist.[6] Among the Moorish Arabs they are held in high esteem as a stimulant, and in Central Arabia they are regarded as a dainty. Their appearance, habits, ravages, etc., are often referred to figuratively in the Scriptures as destructive armies, Nahum iii, 15-17: "Make thyself many as the locusts. * * * Thy crowned are as the locusts and thy marshals as the swarms of grasshoppers, which camp in the hedges in the cold day, but when the sun ariseth they flee away, and their place is not known where they are:"[7] "And the shapes of the locusts were like unto horses prepared for war * * *," etc. In Proverbs xxx, 27, they are enumerated among the "four things which are little upon the earth, but they are exceeding wise." "The locusts have no king, yet they go forth all of them by bands."

MOTH (Hebrew, *Ash, Sas*).—The destructiveness of the moth and its own extreme frailty are often referred to in the Bible as an illustration of the perishable nature of temporal things.[8] "Behold they all shall wax old as a garment; the moth shall eat them up."[9] "Lay not up for

---

[1] II Kings i, 2.
[2] Exodus xxiii, 29; Deuteronomy vii, 20; Joshua xxiv, 12.
[3] Compare Deuteronomy vii, 20; Joshua xxiv, 12.
[4] Exodus x.
[5] Leviticus xi, 20-22.
[6] Matthew iii, 4; Mark i, 6. Compare above under "Pods of the carob tree."
[7] Proverbs xxx, 2; Revelation ix, 7.
[8] Isaiah i, 9.
[9] Matthew vi, 19, 20.

yourselves treasures upon earth, where moth and rust doth consume * * * ."[1] "Your riches are corrupted, and your garments are motheaten."[2] "Whose foundation is in the dust, which are crushed before the moth," and "He buildeth his house as the moth."[3] It is quite plain that at least in most of the passages the *Tineidae*, or clothes moths, are referred to.

PALESTINIAN ANTIQUITIES.

The next group consisted of a selection of objects from the antiquities and art of the peoples who were connected with the history told in the Scriptures. They were put on exhibition for the purpose of enabling the student or visitor to place himself in the position of one who lived in the times and the lands in which the books of the Bible were composed.

Of monuments and relics found in Palestine itself, the following were shown:

CAST OF THE MOABITE STONE.—In II Kings iii it is related that Mesha, the king of Moab, paid tribute to the kings of Israel, but that after the death of Ahab he rebelled. Thereupon Ahab's son, Joram, allied with Jehoshaphat, king of Judah, invaded Moab and shut up Mesha in Kir-Hareseth, situated a little to the east of the southern end of the Dead Sea. Mesha, in this emergency, offered his first born son as a sacrifice, in the presence of the invading army, to Chemosh, the principal divinity of the Moabites; whereupon the Israelites withdrew. Thus far the Biblical account.

In 1868 the Rev. A. F. Klein, a German missionary, discovered at Dhiban, the ruins of Dibon, the ancient capital of Moab,[4] a stone or stela with an inscription celebrating the achievements of Mesha. It was of dark blue basalt, 3 feet 8½ inches high, 2 feet 3½ inches wide, and 1 foot 1.78 inches thick, rounded at both ends and inscribed with thirty-four lines. The stone was in possession of the Beni Humaydah, a wild Arab tribe east of the Jordan. The Arabs, considering the stone so eagerly sought after by Europeans to be possessed of supernatural power, lit a fire under it and then threw cold water upon it, breaking it into fragments, which were distributed as charms among the different families of the tribe. M. Clermont Ganneau, at that time chancellor of the French consulate, had, previous to the breaking of the stone, been so fortunate as to obtain a paper impression of the entire inscription. Afterwards by careful work he succeeded in collecting most of the fragments, so that six-sevenths of the inscription has been preserved and two-thirds of the stone itself is now in the Louvre at Paris.

In the inscription Mesha relates that Omri and Ahab had oppressed the land of Moab for many years, until he recovered several cities from

---

[1] James v, 2.
[2] Job iv, 18, 19.
[3] Job xxvii, 18.
[4] Numbers xxi, 30; xxxii, 34; Isaiah xv, 2.

the Israelites, mentioning Medeba,[1] Ataroth,[2] and Nebo,[3] where he slew 7,000 people and captured Jahaz, which had been built by the King of Israel. At the conclusion he also mentions a battle against Horonaim, which is generally interpreted as referring to a successful war with the Edomites who might have invaded the country from the south. It will thus be seen that the contents of this comparatively brief historical document add considerably to our knowledge of the happenings in the ancient world in the ninth century B. C. The dialect of the inscription differs but slightly from Hebrew, and the characters employed are those of ancient Hebrew, the so-called Samaritan or Phenician. Aside from its historical interest just mentioned, the Moabite stone is the most important surviving relic of the Moabite civilization. It is the oldest monument bearing a Semitic inscription, and its discovery was of great importance for the history of the development of the alphabet, proving, as it does, that the Greeks added nothing to the alphabet which they received from the East.[4]

CAST OF THE SILOAM INSCRIPTION.—The pool or fountain of Siloam, Hebrew, *Shiloah*, i. e., "sending," is mentioned in Isaiah viii, 6; "the waters of Shiloah that go softly"[5] where Jesus sends a blind man to wash in the pool "and he came seeing." It is at the southeast end of Jerusalem and was fed by the waters of a spring of the Gihon, the modern fountain of the Virgin, with which it is connected by a winding tunnel, cut for a distance of 1,708 feet through the solid rock.

The Siloam inscription was accidentally discovered in June, 1880, by a schoolboy, who, while playing with other boys near the pool of Siloam and wading up a channel cut in the rock which leads into the pool, slipped and fell into the water. On rising to the surface he noticed what looked like letters on the wall of the channel; this fact he reported to Mr. Schick, the well-known architect and archæologist of Jerusalem. Mr. Schick announced the discovery to the German Palestine Exploration Society (Deutscher Palaestina Verein), and with much labor made copies during the winter of 1880–81, which were sent to Europe. Owing, however, to the fact that the characters had become filled with a deposit of lime these copies were practically unintelligible.[6]

---

[1] Numbers xxi, 30; Joshua xiii, 9, etc.
[2] Numbers xxxii, 34; Joshua xvi, 2, etc.
[3] Numbers xxxii, 3; Isaiah xv, 2, etc.
[4] The inscription has been translated by Noeldcke, Ginsburg, Ganneau, Schlottmann, W. Hayes Ward, Wright, Smend, and Socin, Die Inschrift des Koenigs Mesa von Moab, Freiburg, 1886, and Canon Driver, Notes on the Hebrew Text of the Books of Samuel, with an Introduction on Hebrew Paleography, and the Ancient Versions and Facsimiles of Inscriptions, Oxford and New York, 1890, pp. lxxxiv–xciv; compare also A. H. Sayce, Fresh Light from the Ancient Monuments, p. 91.
[5] Nehemiah iii, 15, and John ix, 7.
[6] A curious controversy has arisen as to the credit for the work of lowering the level of the water in the channel to render the inscription accessible. Dr. Guthe, in the Zeitschrift der Deutschen Morgenländischen Gesellschaft, XXXVI, p. 726, claims that it was done at the expense of the German Palestine Exploration Society; while the same claim is made for the London Palestine Exploration Fund. Quarterly Statement, 1881, p. 142; 1882, p. 1.

The first legible copies were made by Prof. A. H. Sayce, who came to Jerusalem in February, 1881. He spent three afternoons in the tunnel, sitting in water 4 to 6 inches deep, the conduit being dimly lighted by a candle held by his companion, Mr. Slater.[1] Another copy was independently made by the Rev. W. T. Pilter.

In March, 1881, Dr. Guthe, head of the German Palestine Exploration Society, went to Jerusalem, and after making as exact a drawing as possible of the inscription as it stood, he removed the lime deposit by the application of hydrochloric acid. This rendered feasible the taking of an adequate impression of the inscription. Squeezes and plaster impressions were subsequently made by Dr. Guthe, Lieuts. Claude R. Conder and Mantel.[2]

In 1891 the Siloam inscription was cut out of its place in the tunnel and carried away. It was found in the house of a Greek living near Jerusalem on the Hebron road, and the fact reported to the authorities at Constantinople. The Turkish law makes all monuments public property, and the minister of public instruction ordered the inscription sent to Constantinople. So important, however, was the matter deemed that it was considered at a council of ministers, and a peremptory telegram was sent by the Grand Vizier to the Pasha of Jerusalem to use all means to secure possession of this priceless monument and forward it with dispatch to the capital.[3] This action had the desired result and the Siloam inscription is now preserved at the Imperial Museum in Constantinople.

The contents of the inscription, which consists of six lines, are as follows: "Behold the excavation! And this was the manner of the excavation, while [the excavators] were lifting up the pick, each to his neighbor, and while 3 cubits [of rock remained] the voice of one called to his fellow-workman, for there was a fissure in the rock on the right hand. * * * And on the day [or, to the west] of the excavation the excavators struck, each so as to meet his fellow, pick against pick, and there flowed the water from the source to the pool through the space of 1,000 cubits, and * * * cubit was the height of the rock over the head of the excavation."

The inscription would seem to show that the work of excavation was undertaken simultaneously from both ends by two gangs of workmen, and that for want of engineering skill the borings overlapped.

Judging by the form of the letters the inscription must have originated between the eighth and sixth centuries. The most generally accepted opinion is, that it dates from the reign of Hezekiah, and is referred to in II Chronicles xxxii, 4 and 30: "So there was gathered much people together, and they stopped all the fountains, and the brook that flowed through the midst of the land, saying, why should

---

[1] Quarterly Statement, 1881, p. 143.

[2] Quarterly Statement, 1881, p. 285; 1882, p. 123.

[3] The above account is written from personal knowledge. For a slightly different account see Quarterly Statement, 1891, pp. 2, 88; 1891, pp. 271, 272.

the kings of Assyria come and find much water?" and "This same Hezekiah also stopped the upper springs of the waters of Gihon, and brought them straight down on the west side of the City of David." It is certainly one of the oldest known Hebrew inscriptions.[1]

CAST OF THE LACHISH TABLET.—Lachish was one of the capitals of the Canaanites, situated southeast of Jerusalem, between Gaza and Eleutheropolis. It was conquered by Joshua.[2] The Assyrian King Sennacherib besieged it during his invasion of Judah, 701 B. C.,[3] and, according to the Assyrian inscriptions, captured it. An interesting Assyrian relief represents Sennacherib seated on a throne receiving the tribute of his captives and vassals, accompanied by an inscription containing the statement that the decree was enacted at Lachish. Later on it succumbed to Nebuchadnezzar. The ruins of ancient Lachish, now called Tell el-Hesy, have been explored during the last few years by the Palestine Exploration Fund, and in 1892 Dr. F. Jones Bliss, an American archæologist in charge of the work, discovered there a small clay tablet, inscribed with cuneiform characters, and in a Semitic dialect akin to the Aramaic. The inscription dates before the conquest of Palestine by the Israelites, and contains a letter from the chief of the territory adjoining Lachish, probably to the governor of Lachish, complaining that marauders from the neighboring region are besetting Atim, which is probably identical with Etam, in the south of Judah, mentioned in I Chronicles iv, 32, and Samhi or Sam'a, now probably represented by the large ruin of Sam'ah, 5 miles to the south of Etam. The original is now in possession of the Turkish Government.[4]

CAST OF THE SEAL OF HAGGAI, SON OF SHEBANIAH.—The original seal of black stone was found in 1857 by Sir Charles Warren, near the Haram-esh-Sherif, the mosque of Omar on the site of the temple at Jerusalem.[5] The names Haggai and Shebaniah, which the seal bears, have not been identified. They are possibly connected with the rebuilding of the temple after the exile.

The use of seals or signet rings is already mentioned in the Patriarchal epoch.[6] The seal was either hung on a string around the neck

---

[1] E. J. Pilcher, in the Proceedings of the Biblical Archæology Society, XIX, pp. 165-182, would place the Siloam inscription as late as the time of Herod I (47-4 B. C.); compare, however, the arguments for the usual date of about 700 B. C. by Lieut. Col. C. R. Conder in the Palestine Exploration Quarterly Statement, 1897, pp. 204-208. Compare Idem, 1881, pp. 141-157, 282-297; 1894, pp. 269-277; Canon Driver, Notes on the Hebrew Text of the Books of Samuel, etc., pp. xiv. The "Higher Criticism" and the Verdict of the Monuments by A. H. Sayce, 2d. ed., London, 1894, p. 376.

[2] Joshua x, 3, 31 and 32.

[3] II Kings xviii and xix; Isaiah xxxvi and xxxvii.

[4] A. H. Sayce, Palestine Exploration Fund, Quarterly Statement, 1893, pp. 25-30, and C. R. Conder, The Tell Amarna Tablets, pp. 131-134.

[5] See the Recovery of Jerusalem, by Captain Wilson, R. E., Captain Warren, R. E., with an introduction by Arthur Penrhyn Stanley, edited by Walter Morrison, New York, 1871, pp. 95, 385.

[6] Genesis xxxviii, 18. E. J. Pilcher in the Proceedings of the Society of Biblical Archæology, xix, p. 172, attributes the seal to the time of Herod I (37-4 B. C.), because it was found at the base of the temple wall.

or worn in rings on the finger;[1] "though Coniah, the son of Jehoiakim, King of Judah, were the signet upon my right hand, yet I would pluck thee hence." The seal was used for signing letters and documents.[2] "So she wrote letters in Ahab's name, and sealed them with his seal;" for sealing purses.[3] "My transgression is sealed up in a bag," doors and the like.[4] "So they went and made the sepulchre sure, sealing the stone." The custom of making an impression with the seal upon the forehead of a person is alluded to in the Epistle to the Galatians vi, 17: "I bear branded on my body the marks of Jesus," and Revelations vii, 3 and 4: "Hurt not the earth, neither the sea, nor the trees, till we shall have sealed the servants of our God on their foreheads."

BIBLICAL WEIGHTS.—The weights (like the measures) of the Hebrews are usually traced to the Babylonian system, which is considered the parent of other oriental systems. The unit of the Hebrew weights was the *shekel;* the other weights were either its multiples or fractions. The weights mentioned in the Bible are as follows: Talent[5] (*kikkar*), equals 60 minas or 3,600 shekels, equal to about 674,000 grains Troy; mina[6] (*maneh*), equals 60 shekels, equal to about 11,000 grains Troy; shekel (*sheqel*), equal to about 220 grains, one-twentieth (*gerah*) of a shekel,[7] or about 11 grains.[8] Scales, *mo'znayim*, consisted of a beam resting at its central point on a standard, and having suspended from its two ends two scales or basins in which the weights and the substances to be weighed were placed respectively.[9] Alongside of the *moznayim* there is also mentioned *peles*,[10] which is assumed to answer to the modern steelyard, also called Roman balance or beam, consisting of a lever in the form of a slender iron bar with one arm very short, the other divided by equidistant notches, having a small cross piece as a fulcrum to which a bearing for suspension is attached, usually a hook at the short end, and a weight moving upon the long arm. The weights themselves were called in the Hebrew "stones," rendered "weights" in the English versions.

CAST OF AN ANCIENT HEBREW WEIGHT.—The original, which is of hematite, was obtained by Dr. Th. Chaplin, in Samaria. The weight is spindle shaped, somewhat flattened on one side, and weighs about 40 grains. It has on both sides a Hebrew legend, which is interpreted to mean "Quarter of a quarter of neçeg," which may have been a standard weight in Palestine.[11]

---

[1] Jeremiah xxii, 24.
[2] I Kings xxi, 8.
[3] Job xiv, 17.
[4] Matthew xxvii, 66.
[5] I Kings ix, 14; x, 10, 14; II Kings v, 23. Compare Matthew xviii, 24.
[6] Ezekiel xlv, 12.
[7] Exodus xxx, 13; Leviticus xxvii, 25; Ezekiel xlv, 12.
[8] Psalms lxii, 9; Proverbs xi, 1; xvi, 11; xx, 23; Job vi, 2; xxxi, 6.
[9] E. C. Bissell, Biblical Antiquities, Philadelphia, 1888.
[10] Isaiah xl, 12; Proverbs xvi, 11.
[11] Palestine Exploration Fund, Quarterly Statement, 1890, p. 267; 1894, pp. 220-231, 284-287.

CAST OF A BEAD.—The original, a reddish perforated yellow stone, was obtained by Prof. T. F. Wright, in Jerusalem. It weighs 134 grains, and is inscribed with the word neçeg in the same characters as those of the Siloam inscription. It was probably used as a weight, and the inscription may mean "standard weight."[1]

MUSICAL INSTRUMENTS.

As of great general interest for the history of culture there was shown a collection of musical instruments mentioned in the Bible, supplemented by photographs and casts of representations of musical instruments on ancient monuments. Scarcely any authentic information is preserved concerning the shape or the manner of playing on the musical instruments named in the Bible. The instruments exhibited were such as are now in use in the Oriental countries. But it may be assumed that the musical instruments of the Hebrews resembled those of the nations with which they came in contact, and that, considering the stability and conservatism of the East, the instruments still used in Palestine, Syria, and Egypt differ but little, if at all, from those employed in ancient times.

It is well known that music occupies an important place in the Bible. Its invention is recorded in the opening chapters of the Scriptures, where Jubal is named as the "father (i. e., founder) of all such as handle the harp and pipe."[2] From the earliest times music was of high importance among the Israelites, accompanying all the great national events and adorning the festal occasions. The hymn of thanksgiving after the deliverance from the bondage of Egypt and the passing through the Red Sea[3] was accompanied by the sound of timbrels and by dances of a choir of women led by the prophetess Miriam.[4] The solemnity of the giving of the law on Sinai was enhanced by the sound of the horn or *shofar*,[5] and the same instrument is mentioned at the capture of Jericho, the first conquest made in the Promised Land.[6] The sound of trumpets and of the horn announced and inaugurated the great festivals and the year of "Jubilee."[7]

But music also permeated the common daily life in Israel, and the absence of the "mirth of tabrets" and the "joy of the harp" was one of the signs of a national calamity.[8] It was the pastime of the shepherd;[9] it formed the principal attraction of the social gatherings of youth at the city gates;[10] it heightened the mirth at the festivals of the harvest

---

[1] Palestine Exploration Fund, Quarterly Statement, 1893, pp. 32, 257.
[2] Hebrew, *Kinnor* and *Ugab*, Genesis iv, 21.
[3] Exodus xv.
[4] Verse 20.
[5] Exodus xix, 16, 19.
[6] Joshua vi, 5.
[7] Numbers x, 10; xxix, 1; Leviticus xxv, 8, 9.
[8] Isaiah xxiv, 8; Lamentation v, 14.
[9] I Samuel xvi, 18.
[10] Lamentation v, 14.

and vintage;[1] it contributed to the pleasure and festivity of the banquet;[2] the victors in battle were received on their return with "singing, dancing, and timbrels."[3] In short, music seems to have been the indispensable accompaniment of every public occasion, whether joyous or sad.[4]

But it was in religious worship that music attained its highest development in Israel, and it is to the time of David that the extensive use of music in religious service, both vocal and instrumental, was ascribed. From the 38,000 Levites 4,000 were elected and organized under 288 leaders into a chorus and orchestra to provide for the music of the sanctuary. The 288 classes were separated into 42 divisions under the sons of Asaph, Jeduthun, and Heman, as masters, and the entire chorus and orchestra was under the direction of Asaph, Jeduthun, and Heman.[5] These sanctuary musicians also officiated at the dedication of the temple by Solomon.[6] Under the later idolatrous kings it may be assumed that the music, like the worship of the temple, was often neglected. It is, on the other hand, especially mentioned that the pious kings, Hezekiah and Josiah, gave much attention to the musical services of the temple.[7] It was employed at the restoration of the temple and the walls of Jerusalem after the return from the exile;[8] and from post-biblical writings, especially Josephus, it is known that it continued to form a prominent feature of Jewish worship.

The musical instruments mentioned in the Bible may be divided, after the usual classifications, into the following groups:

(1) Instruments of percussion, which were beaten or shaken to produce sound for the purpose of regulating the rhythmic element in music. These instruments were presumably the first used, and are still common among the less cultivated peoples.

(2) Wind instruments.

(3) String instruments, which were always played with the fingers or with the plectrum, and not, like the modern violin, with a bow.

Of the instruments mentioned in the Bible, two—the ram's horn and the trumpet—are commanded to be used for sacred purposes.[9] These two instruments are also the only ones concerning whose shape there is absolute certainty.

Of the trumpet there is a representation extant on the Arch of Titus at Rome, while there is no doubt that the ram's horn which is still used in the synagogue has conserved its antique form.[10]

---

[1] Isaiah xvi, 10.
[2] Isaiah v, 12; Amos vi, 5; II Samuel xix, 35.
[3] Exodus xv, 21; Judges xi, 34; I Samuel xviii, 6.
[4] Genesis xxxi, 27; Luke xv, 25; II Chronicles xxxv, 25; Matthew ix, 23; Jeremiah ix, 17, 18, and 19.
[5] I Chronicles xxiii, 5; xxv, 7.
[6] II Chronicles v, 12, 13.
[7] II Chronicles xxix, 25; xxxv, 15.
[8] Ezra iii, 10, 11; Nehemiah xi, 17, 22; xii, 28.
[9] Leviticus xxiii, 24; xxv, 9; Numbers x, 2.
[10] Johann Weiss, Die musikalischen Instrumente in den Heiligen Schriften des Alten Testamentes, Gratz, 1895.

EXPLANATION OF PLATE 1.

```
┌─────────────────────┐
│  1      3           │
│              5      │
│  2      4           │
└─────────────────────┘
```

Fig. 1. CASTANETS.
 (Cat. No. 95174, U. S. N. M. Beirut, Syria. Collected by Erhard Bessinger, U. S. Consul.)
Fig. 2. CYMBALS (*meciltayim*).
 (Cat. No. 95173, U. S. N. M. Cairo, Egypt. Collected by Louis B. Grant, U. S. Vice-Consul.)
Fig. 3. ROUND TABRET (*tof*).
 (Cat. No. 95151, U. S. N. M. Beirut, Syria. Collected by Erhard Bissinger, U. S. Consul.)
Fig. 4. FOUR-SIDED TABRET.
 (Cat. No. 95779, U. S. N. M. Morocco, Africa. Collected by Dr. Talcott Williams.)
Fig. 5. KETTLE-DRUM.
 (Cat. No. 95175, U. S. N. M. Cairo, Egypt. Collected by Louis B. Grant, U. S. Vice-Consul.)

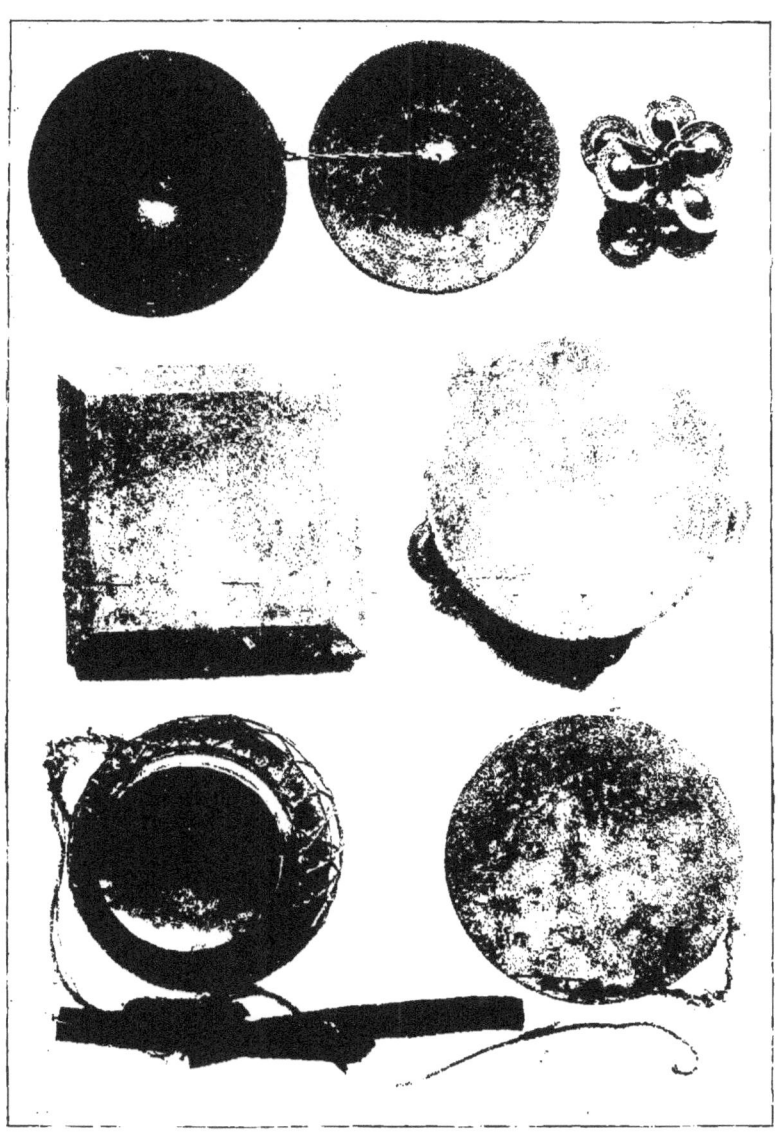

MUSICAL INSTRUMENTS OF PERCUSSION.

The instruments exhibited, of which illustrations are given here, were as follows:

I.—INSTRUMENTS OF PERCUSSION.

(1) ROUND TABRET, HAND-DRUM (Hebrew, *Tof*).—From Beirut, Syria, where it is called *rikk*. (See plate 1, fig. 3.) The Arabic name *duff* agrees with the Hebrew, and is the parent of the Spanish *aduffa*.

The tabret or timbrel is mentioned in Genesis xxxi, 27. Its use survived from the earliest time to the present day in Asia, Greece, and Italy. On old Grecian monuments the tabret is seen in the hands of Bacchantes and priests of Cybele. On the Egyptian sculptures two forms of the tabret are represented, the round and the four-sided. The use of the striker seems not to have been known in antiquity. The tabret was beaten with the hand and was suspended from the neck by a ribbon. Later modifications of the tabret resemble our drum and the kettle-drum. The use of the tabret was confined to joyous occasions. It served with other instruments of song[1] to accentuate the rhythm of the dance.[2] It was played mostly by women, accompanying the harp and lute, at joyous feasts,[3] at the reception of victorious generals,[4] at banquets,[5] and at weddings.[6] In solemn processions it was also played by men.[7] The tabret is not mentioned among the instruments used in the religious services of the tabernacle or temple.

(2) FOUR-SIDED TABRET, Morocco, Africa. (See plate 1, fig. 4.)

(3) KETTLEDRUM (Arabic, *Naggarah*), Cairo, Egypt. (See plate 1, fig. 5.)—The kettledrum is made either of wood or copper, one side being rounded, the other flat, on which the skin (of a goat or gazelle) is stretched. It is now used in military bands, orchestras, and short solo passages. It is also employed by the dervishes to produce excitement in their devotions. The kettledrum is sounded with blows from a soft-headed, elastic mallet, stick, or a leather thong.

(4) CYMBALS (Hebrew, *Meçiltayim*, *Çelçelím*). (See plate 1, fig. 2.) These two Hebrew words, which are usually considered identical, are plainly onomatopoeic. Though it is hardly likely that they indicated the same instrument, we have at present no certain method of differentiating them. *Meçiltayim* is almost invariably in the dual form, which indicates two similar parts, and in one passage[8] the material of which they were made, copper or brass, is named. Cymbals are mentioned only in connection with religious ceremonies.[9]

---

[1] Genesis xxxi, 27; Psalms lxxxi, 2.
[2] Exodus xv, 20; Judges xi, 34; I Samuel xviii, 6; Jeremiah xxxi, 4; Psalms cl, 4.
[3] Isaiah xxiv, 8; xxx, 32; Job xxi, 12.
[4] Judges xi, 34; I Samuel xviii, 6.
[5] Isaiah v, 12.
[6] I Maccabees ix, 39.
[7] II Samuel vi, 5, and I Chronicles xiii, 8.
[8] I Chronicles xv, 19.
[9] II Samuel vi, 5; I Chronicles xiii, 8; xv, 16, 19, 28; xvi, 5, 42; xxv, 1, 6; II Chronicles v, 12, 13; xxix, 25; Ezra iii, 10; Nehemiah xii, 27; Psalms cl, 5.

The cymbals now used in the Orient are much like those depicted on the Egyptian and Assyrian monuments. They consisted of two large plates of metal with wide, flat rims, and were played by being strapped to the hands and clashed together. Others were conical, or cup-like, with thin edges, and were played by bringing down the one sharply on the other, while held stationary, eliciting a high-pitched note. Cymbals were made of brass, and it is probable that they were the first among musical instruments made of metal. They were represented by a specimen from Cairo, Egypt, called by the Arabs *Ka's*.

(5) CASTANETS.—(See plate 1, fig. 1.) Some scholars apply the Hebrew names for cymbals. *Çelçelim* and *Meçiltayim*, which denote a jingling sound, also to castanets; others think these are meant by the *Çilçele-stema* (R. V. "Loud cymbals") Psalms cl, 5. But this is by no means certain.

II.—WIND INSTRUMENTS.

(1) RAM'S HORN (Hebrew, *Shofar*). (See plate 2, fig. 2.)—The Shofar, in the English versions usually inaccurately translated trumpet, or even more inaccurately cornet, is first mentioned in the Bible in connection with the giving of the law on Sinai.[1] Its use is ordered in the Pentateuch for the announcement of the new moon and solemn feasts[2] and the proclamation of the year of release.[3] New Year's Day (the first of the seventh month, or *Tishri*) is called a "memorial day of blowing."[4] The *Shofar* also served in religious processions,[5] and is mentioned, along with other musical instruments as a proper accompaniment of psalmody: "Praise Him with the blowing of the shofar, praise Him with the psaltery and harp."[6] But the most ancient and most frequent use of the shofar was for military purposes, to give the signal for the rallying of the people and for attacking and pursuing the enemy. Animal horns were similarly used in the Roman army.[7] The shofar is not only the sole instrument of those mentioned in the Bible which is still employed by the Jews in their religious services of the synagogue during the penitential month of *Elul* (July-August), on New Year's Day, or *Rosh ha-Shanah*, the first of *Tishri* (August-September), and on Atonement Day, or *Yom Kippur*, the tenth of *Tishri*, but is also, according to authorities on musical instruments, the oldest form of wind instrument known to be retained in use. It is usually made of a ram's horn, though the goat's horn is also employed.[8]

---

[1] Exodus xix. 16; xx, 18.
[2] Numbers x. 10; compare Psalms lxxxi, 4.
[3] Leviticus xxv, 9.
[4] Leviticus xxiii, 24; Number xxix, 1.
[5] II Samuel vi. 15; I Chronicles xv, 28.
[6] Psalms cl. 3; compare xcviii, 6.
[7] Varro, De lingua Latina v, 117; ea (cornua) quae nunc sunt ex aere, tunc fiebant e bubulo cornu.
[8] Cyrus Adler. "The Shofar, its use and origin (Proc. U. S. Nat. Mus., XVI, pp. 287-301; Report U. S. Nat. Mus., 1892, pp. 437-450).

EXPLANATION OF PLATE 2.

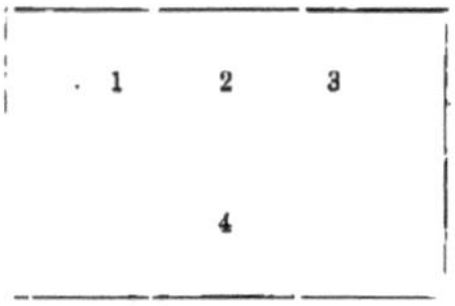

.1	2	3
	4	

Fig. 1. REEDS OR PAN PIPES.
    (Cat. No. 95705, U. S. N. M. Cairo, Egypt. Collected by Dr. G. Brown Goode.)
Fig. 2. RAM'S HORN (*shofar*).
    (Cat. No. 95142, U. S. N. M. Deposited by Dr. Cyrus Adler.)
Fig. 3. DOUBLE FLUTE.
    (Cat. No. 95654, U. S. N. M. Bethlehem, Palestine. Collected by Dr. G. Brown Goode.)
Fig. 4. FLUTE (*halil*).
    (Cat. No. 95695, U. S. N. M. Damascus, Syria. Collected by Dr. G. Brown Goode.)

National Museum, 1896 — Adler and Casanowicz.

PLATE 2

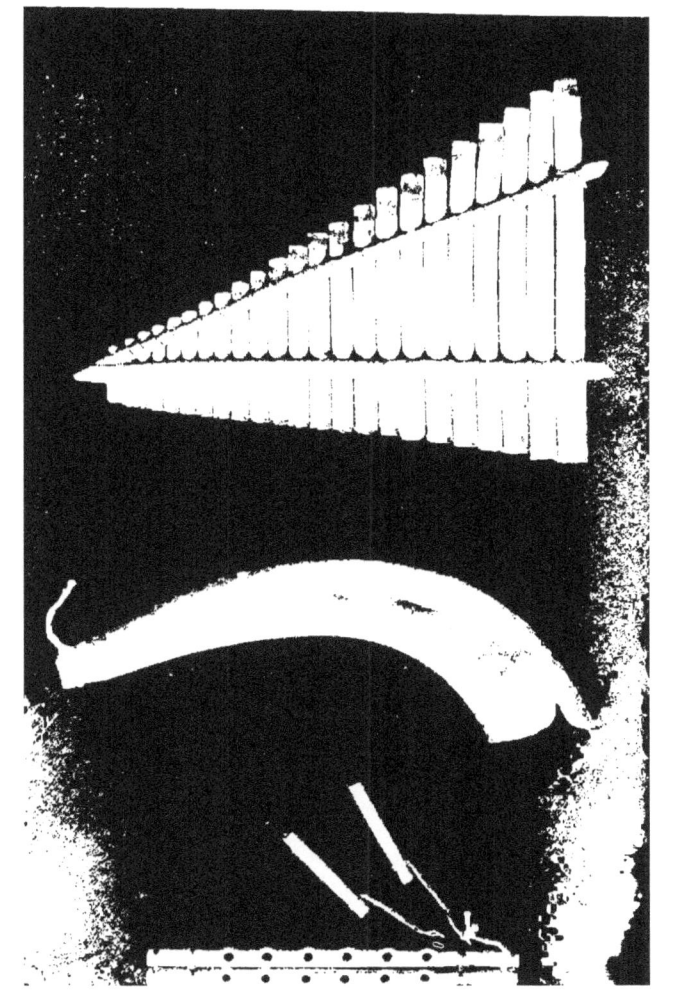

(2) TRUMPET (Hebrew, *Haçoçerah*), Morocco, where it is called *n'feer*. (See plate 3.)—The trumpet was expressly designed in the Pentateuch for sacred uses, two being ordered to be made of silver,[1] while Solomon increased their number to one hundred and twenty.[2] It was almost exclusively a priestly instrument.[3] Its primary use was for giving signals for the people to assemble.[4] Later it was appropriated to religious services[5] and festive occasions.[6] According to the representation on the Arch of Titus, the trumpet was narrow and straight, with a ball-like protuberance at the bottom. It was represented by its modern survival, the *n'feer* of Morocco. The instrument itself was supplemented by a photograph of the Arch of Titus. (See plate 5.)

(3) FLUTE OR PIPE (Hebrew, *Halil;* Revised Version, flute.) Damascus, Syria. (See plate 2, fig. 4.) The pipe or flute, now called in Syria *Shubab*, was a favorite instrument of the ancients. In its simplest form it was a reed or variety of wood in the shape of a reed, about 18 inches in length, bored throughout evenly, and pierced with holes in the sides for notes. Later, even ivory was employed. A variety of flutes are exhibited in the representations of Egyptian, Oriental, and Grecian musical instruments. They may be divided into simple flutes, which were either direct or transverse double flutes with even or uneven tubes, and those with several tubes.

The invention of the simple flute is ascribed by the Greeks to the Egyptians;[7] that of the transverse flute likewise to the Egyptians,[8] or to the Lybians.[9] The double flute is seen on Egyptian and Assyrian monuments. Among the Greeks and Romans the flute was played by the Bacchants, at funerals, and also at festive banquets. The Lacedaemonians, Cretans, and Lybians used it also for military purposes. In the Bible the flute is not mentioned among the musical instruments of the Temple; but it was employed on various festal occasions—at the accession of Solomon to the throne[10] and other festivities,[11] as well as at funerals.[12] According to post-Biblical sources of information, flutes were used in the daily service of the second temple.[13]

(4) DOUBLE FLUTE, Bethlehem, Palestine. (See plate 2, fig. 3.) This instrument is assumed by some to represent the *Sumponiah* (sym-

---

[1] Numbers x, 1-10.
[2] II Chronicles v, 12.
[3] Numbers x, 2-10; xxxi, 6; II Chronicles xiii, 12, 14.
[4] See Numbers x, 5, 6, where the manner of blowing is specified, so as to indicate the different signals intended.
[5] II Kings xii, 13; II Chronicles xiii, 12, 14.
[6] Psalms xcviii, 6; Ezra iii, 10; II Kings xi, 14; II Chronicles xxiii, 13.
[7] Athenæus IV, p. 175.
[8] *Idem*, p. 185.
[9] Pollux, IV, 84.
[10] I Kings i, 40.
[11] I Samuel x, 5; Isaiah xxx, 29; Revelation xviii, 22.
[12] Matthew ix, 23.
[13] Talmud Erachin, 10a; Tacitus, Historiæ, v, 5.

phony) in Daniel iii, 5, 10, 15. The Authorized and Revised Versions give dulcimer, though the margin of the latter gives bagpipe. Engel[1] says that the Italian peasantry still call a bagpipe *Zampogna*, and according to the last edition of Gesenius *Sambonjo* and *Zampogna* have also persisted in Asia Minor. *Sumponiah* is supposed by some to be a translation of the Hebrew *'ugab*, though the latter possibly represents pan pipes.

(5) REEDS OR PAN PIPES, Cairo, Egypt. (See plate 2, fig. 1.) The reeds now called in Egypt *safafir* are probably the Hebrew *'ugab*.[2] They were known to the Greeks under the name of *syrinx* (Latin *fistula*). There was shown in addition to the Egyptian instrument an Assyrian bas-relief representing a flute player. (See plate 3.)

(6) BAGPIPE, represented by an instrument from Tunis, Africa, where it is called *zaida*, possibly Aramaic *Sumponiah* mentioned in Daniel iii, 5, 10. (See plate 6.) The bagpipe originated in the East, and was known to the Greeks and Romans.[3] It was popular throughout the middle ages and is still used in many eastern countries and among the country people of Poland, Italy, the south of France, and in Scotland and Ireland.

III.—STRINGED INSTRUMENTS.

(1) HARP.—The Hebrew word *Kinnor*, which is adopted for harp, occurs in the opening chapters of the Bible.[4] It was the especial instrument of David.[5] Later it was one of the important instruments of the Temple orchestra,[6] being one of the instruments most frequently mentioned in the Bible.[7] To judge from representations on Egyptian monuments and Jewish coins of the second century B. C., the *Kinnor* resembled the Greek *Kithara* more than the modern trigonal harp, a theory corroborated by the fact that the Hebrew *Kinnor* is usually rendered *Kithara* ($\kappa\iota\theta\acute{a}\rho a$) by the Septuagint, the oldest Greek version of the Old Testament. Jewish coins show lyres with three, five, and six strings.

A similar instrument was also in use among the Assyrians. In its smaller form it could easily be carried about in processions, as the representations on the monuments, both Egyptian and Assyrian, show. (A photograph of a relief of an Assyrian harp player was exhibited. See plate 7.)

(2) PSALTERY OR DULCIMER (Hebrew, *Nebel*). (See plate 8.) Next to the harp (*kinnor*) and mostly in conjunction with it, the psaltery is

---

[1] Musical Instruments, p. 23.
[2] Genesis iv, 21.
[3] It was introduced in Rome in the imperial period under the name of *tibia utricularis* or *chorus* and soon obtained great popularity. (Compare Seneca, Epistol, 76.)
[4] Genesis iv, 21.
[5] I Samuel xvi, 23.
[6] I Chronicles xv, 16; II Chronicles xxix. 25.
[7] Genesis xxxi, 27; Isaiah xxiii, 16; Psalms xxxiii, 2; xliii, 4; Job xxi, 12.

TRUMPET.
Morocco, Africa.
Cat. No. 95289, U.S.N.M. Collected by Dr. Talcott Williams.

National Museum, 1896.—Adler and Casanowicz.

ASSYRIAN BAS-RELIEF REPRESENTING A FLUTE PLAYER.
Original in Royal Museum, Berlin.
Cat. No. 130213, U.S.N.M.

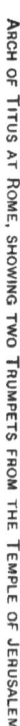

Arch of Titus at Rome, showing two trumpets from the Temple of Jerusalem.

BAGPIPE.
Tunis, Africa.
Cat. No. 95141, U.S.N.M. Collected by Dr. Cyrus Adler.

ASSYRIAN BAS-RELIEF SHOWING HARP PLAYERS.
Original in British Museum.
Collection U. S. National Museum.

HITTITE LUTE PLAYER.
Senjirli, Asia Minor.
Original in Royal Museum, Berlin.
Cat. No. 155045, U.S.N.M.

most frequently mentioned in the Bible. It is likely that the psaltery resembled what is now known in the East as the tamboora or guitar, an instrument which also figures largely on the Egyptian and Assyrian monuments. In its present shape the psaltery is thus described: "In its most complete and perfect form this instrument is 3 feet 9 inches long, has ten strings of fine wire and forty-seven stops. It is played with a plectrum, and is often inlaid with mother-of-pearl and valuable woods. It is oftener, however, of smaller size and less costly materials."[1] Others assume that the *nebel* resembled the harp-shaped instruments seen on Assyrian monuments. In Psalms xxxiii, 2, *nebel asor*, the "*nebel* of ten," probably ten strings, is mentioned. This would curiously agree in detail with the instrument described above. Engel[2] assumes that there is an independent instrument called the *asor*, which is supported by Psalms xcii, 3, "with an instrument of ten strings, and with the psaltery."[3]

PRECIOUS STONES OF THE BIBLE.

The use of precious stones for ornament, as well as with engraving for signets and the like, was well known to all of the Mediterranean peoples, and quite a goodly number of them are mentioned in the Bible.

The engraving of signets upon hard stones was practiced at an early period. The Israelites may have acquired the art from the Egyptians, who are known to have made use of the lapidary's wheel and emery powder, and are supposed to have been acquainted with the diamond and the method of engraving other stones by means of it. The Assyrians and Babylonians were very skillful in engraving on gems, many of which have been found in the ruins of their palaces and cities.

The sources for the names of gems in the Bible are three almost identical lists:

I. The description of the High Priest's "breastplate of judgment" (*hoshen ha-mishpat*), in which were placed, in gold setting, four rows of precious stones, three in each row, engraved with the names of the twelve tribes of Israel.[4]

II. The description of the ornaments of the King of Tyre.[5]

III. The description of the foundation of the Heavenly City.[6]

In many instances the exact equivalent of the biblical names of precious stones is uncertain in the nomenclature of modern mineralogy. In the following tables are given, alongside of the original and the Septuagint, the meaning adopted by most authorities, the rendering

---

[1] Van Lennep, Bible Lands, p. 612.

[2] Musical Instruments, p. 19.

[3] Compare on the subject of music of the ancient Hebrews the excellent appendix to the Psalms in Prof. Paul Haupt's Polychrome Edition of the Bible, pp. 217-231, 236, 237.

[4] Exodus xxviii, 17-20.

[5] Ezekiel xxviii, 13.

[6] Revelations xxi, 19, 20.

of the Revised Version, both in the text and margin, being added in parentheses.

Besides the stones enumerated in these lists, there are probably mentioned, first, diamond, Hebrew *shamir*, for which the following passages serve as illustrations: Jeremiah xvii, 1: "The sin of Judah is written with a pen of iron, and with the point of a diamond;" Ezekiel iii, 9: "As an adamant harder than flint have I made thy forehead;" Zechariah vii, 12: "Yea, they made their hearts as an adamant stone, lest they should hear the law;" second, amber (margin of Revised Version, following the Septuagint and Vulgate, electrum), Hebrew, *hashmal*, Ezekiel i, 4, which however, may represent some metallic compound, possibly the mixture of gold and silver, now called electrum; and, third, crystal, Hebrew *qerah* and *gabish*, properly ice, according to the view of the ancients, that crystal was ice hardened by intense cold.[1]

The three lists of precious stones in the Bible.

I. EXODUS XXVIII, 17-20.

1. *Odem* (*sardion*), carnelian (sardius, ruby).	2. *Pitdah* (*topazion*), topaz or peridot.	3. *Bareketh* (*smaragdos*), smaragd or emerald (carbuncle emerald).
4. *Nofek* (*anthrax*), carbuncle, probably the Indian ruby (emerald, carbuncle).	5. *Sappir* (*sapfeiros*), sapphire or lapis lazuli (sapphire).	6. *Yahalom* (*iaspis*), onyx, a kind of chalcedon (diamond, sardonyx).
7. *Leshem** (*ligyrion*), jacinth, others, sapphire (jacinth, amber).	8. *Shebo* (*achates*), agate.	9. *Achlamah** (*amethystos*), amethyst.
10. *Tarshish* (*chrysolithos*), chrysolite, others, topaz, (beryl, chalcedony).	11. *Shoham* (*beryllion*), beryl (onyx, beryl).	12. *Yashpeh* (*onychion*), jasper.

II. EZEKIEL XXVIII, 13.

1. *Odem*.	2. *Pitdah*.	3. *Yahalom*.
4. *Tarshish*.	5. *Shoham*.	6. *Yashpeh*.
7. *Sappir*.	8. *Nofek*.	9. *Bareketh*.

III. REVELATIONS XXI, 19, 20.

1. *Iaspis*, jasper.	2. *Sapfeiros*, sapphire or lapis lazuli.	3. *Chalkedon*, chalcedony.
4. *Smaragdos*, smaragd (emerald).	5. *Sardonyx*, sardonyx.	6. *Sardios*, sardius.
7. *Chrysolithos*, chrysolite.	8. *Beryllos*, beryl.	9. *Topazion*, topaz.
10. *Chrysoprasos*, chrysoprase.	11. *Hyakinthos*, jacinth (margin, sapphire).	12. *Amethystos*, amethyst.

*Dr. Fr. Hommel, in his book, The Ancient Hebrew Tradition as Illustrated by the Monuments New York, 1897, p. 281, compare also p. 291, surmises that *leshem* and *achlamah* are Egyptian loanwords, derived respectively from the Egyptian names *neshem* and *ekhnóme*.

[1] Ezekiel i, 22; Job xxviii, 18; Revelations iv, 6.

EXPLANATION OF PLATE 9.

```
 1   2   3   4   5   6
 7   8
     9  10  11  12  13
14  15  16  17  18  19  20  21
22  23      24              28
    25  26      27
```

Fig. 1. SHEKEL.
Fig. 2. COIN OF HEROD AGRIPPA II.
Fig. 3. COINS OF JOHN HYRCANUS.
Fig. 4. COIN OF ALEXANDER JANNÆUS (*widow's mite*).
Fig. 5. STATERS OF ANTIOCH.
Fig. 6. COIN OF HEROD ANTIPAS.
Fig. 7. COIN OF HEROD PHILIP.
Fig. 8. COIN OF CÆSAREA.
Fig. 9. TETRADRACHM OF SIDON.
Fig. 10. COINS OF DAMASCUS.
Fig. 11. COIN OF ASKELON.
Fig. 12. DENARII.
Figs. 13, 14. TETRADRACHMS OF TYRE.
Fig. 15. TETRADRACHM OF ALEXANDER THE GREAT.
Fig. 16. TETRADRACHM OF BABYLON.
Fig. 17. TETRADRACHM OF SELEUCUS I NICATOR.
Fig. 18. STATER OF TARSUS.
Fig. 19. COIN OF DEMETRIUS SOTER.
Fig. 20. COIN OF CYPRUS.
Fig. 21. AES OF THESSALONICA.
Fig. 22. COIN OF THESSALONICA.
Fig. 23. TETRADRACHMS OF ATHENS.
Fig. 24. DIDRACHMS OF ATHENS.
Fig. 25. TETRADRACHMS OF EPHESUS.
Fig. 26. HEMIDRACHMS OF EPHESUS.
Fig. 27. TETRADRACHMS OF MACEDONIA.
Fig. 28. CHILD'S BANK.

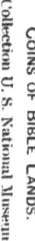

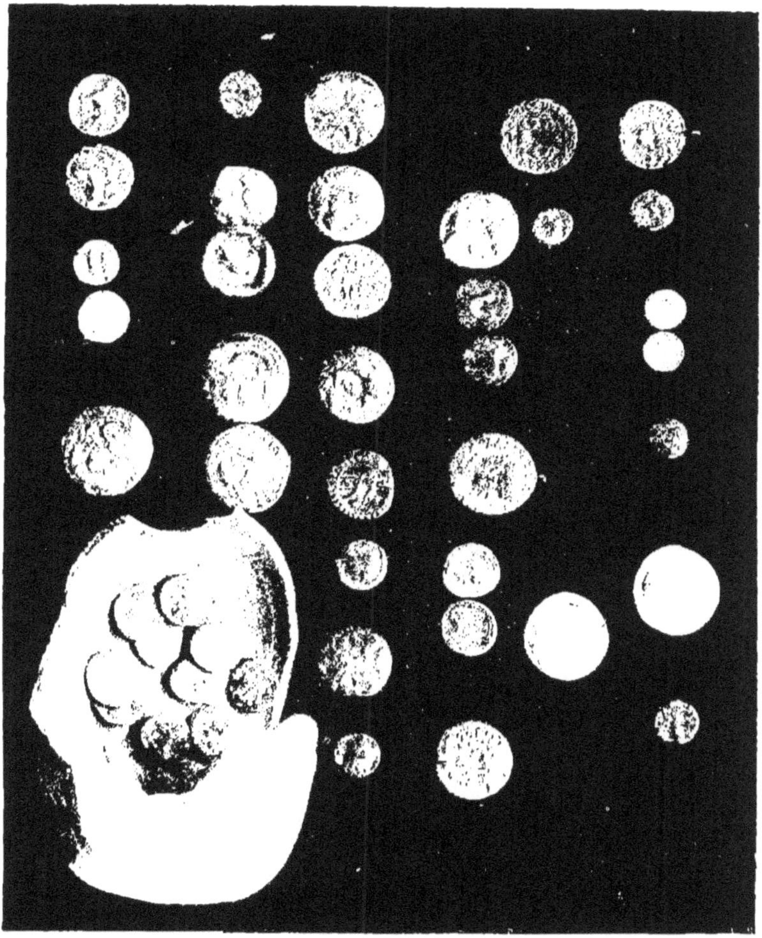

COINS OF BIBLE LANDS.
Collection U. S. National Museum.

The precious stones exhibited were as follows:

RUBY, a variety of corundum (five specimens).—Ruby is given on the margin of the Revised Version for the Hebrew *odem*, which is also, however, rendered carnelian by some authorities. The Hebrew name indicates reddish stone.[1]

TOPAZ.—Topaz is the probable rendering of Hebrew *pitdah*, mentioned in the book of Job (xxviii, 19) as coming from Ethiopia.

GARNET CARBUNCLE (seven specimens).—Carbuncle is given on the margin of the Revised Version for the Hebrew *nofek* and in the text for the Revised Version for *bareqeth*.[2]

EMERALD.—Given in the text of the Revised Version for the Hebrew *nofek*, and in the margin for Hebrew *bareqeth* and Greek *smaragdos*.

SAPPHIRE, a variety of corundum (four specimens).—Hebrew *sappir* and Greek *sapfeiros* are identical with the English name, which is the same as that in all modern languages. Some, however, assume that these names in the Bible signify lapis lazuli.

SARDONYX, a variety of quartz (two specimens).—Sardonyx is given on the margin of the Revised Version for Hebrew *yahalom*.[2]

DIAMOND (one specimen).—The Hebrew *yahalom* in the High Priest's breastplate, Exodus xxviii, 18, is rendered "diamond" in the English version and by Luther. But the diamond could not have been used in the breastplate, because the Hebrews knew of no means of engraving a name upon it. In all probability, however, the diamond is understood by Hebrew *shamir*, Jeremiah xvii, 1; Ezekiel iii, 9; Zechariah vii, 12, where it is spoken of as an object used for engraving, and of extreme hardness.

WHITE SAPPHIRE ADAMANT, a variety of corundum (two specimens).

JACINTH (three specimens).—Jacinth is assumed by some to be the Hebrew *leshem*.

AGATE, a variety of quartz (three specimens).—Agate is agreed to be the Hebrew *shebo*.

AMETHYST, a variety of quartz (three specimens).—Amethyst renders the Hebrew *ahlamah*. It is so called in Greek because it was thought to be a charm against drunkenness. The Hebrews popularly derived it from *halam*, to dream, and supposed that it brought pleasant dreams. Other etymologies have, however, been proposed.

BERYL (two specimens).—Beryl is given for the Hebrew *tarshish*, Revised Version text, and *shoham*, Revised Version margin.

CHALCEDONY, a variety of quartz (six specimens).—One of the stones enumerated in the description of the foundation of the Heavenly City (Revelation xxi, 19). Some assume that *tarshish* in the High Priest's breastplate (Exodus xxviii, 20), means chalcedony. (So the Revised Version margin.) Topaz is also given for this stone.

---

[1] Where no references are given to these names, it may be assumed that they occur in the passages in Exodus, Ezekiel, and Revelations mentioned above.

[2] Exodus xxviii, 18.

ONYX, a variety of quartz.—Given in the Revised Version of the Hebrew *shoham*. *Shohams* set in gold were put on each of the two shoulderstraps of the *ephod* of the High Priest, and the two together had engraved the names of the tribes of Israel (Exodus xxviii, 12). It is mentioned in Genesis ii, 12, in the account of the Garden of Eden.

JASPER, a variety of quartz (two specimens).—This is the accepted meaning of the Hebrew name *yashpeh*, the words being probably identical in origin.

CARNELIAN, a variety of quartz (three specimens).—Possibly Hebrew *odem* of the High Priest's breastplate (Exodus xxviii, 17), and the *sardius* in Revelation iv, 3; xxi, 20.

CHRYSOLITE (two specimens).—Possibly Hebrew *tarshish*.

AMBER (two specimens).—Probably the Hebrew *hashmal* (Ezekiel i, 4). Some suppose that amber is understood by Hebrew *leshem*.

CHRYSOPRASE, a variety of quartz (four specimens).—Enumerated in the description of the foundation of the Heavenly City (Revelation xxi, 20).

LAPIS LAZULI (Persia).—Some authorities suppose that by *sappir* not sapphire but lapis lazuli is meant.

PEARL.—It is supposed by some that the pearl is meant by the Hebrew *peninim*, which is often employed in the Old Testament as a figure of something valuable and precious.[1]

In addition to the gems there was also exhibited a silver breastplate, used as an ornament for the manuscript copy of the Pentateuch (*Torah*) employed in the synagogue, which represented the twelve stones which were set in the breastplate of the High Priest[2] with the names of the twelve tribes of Israel underneath them.

A SELECTION OF THE COINS OF BIBLE LANDS.

(Plate 9.)

Coined money did not circulate among the Israelites previous to their return from the Babylonian captivity, and indeed there is no evidence that it did then. It is unquestioned, however, that specific weights of gold and silver were well recognized in commercial transactions from a very early period.[3] This was principally silver in the form of bars—ingots—translated in the authorized and revised versions

---

[1] Proverbs iii, 15; xxxi, 10; Job xxviii, 18. Jesus uses the pearl for the same purpose (Matthew vii, 6; xiii, 45): "Give not that which is holy unto the dogs, neither cast your pearls before swine, lest haply they trample them under their feet, and turn and rend you." Again, "The Kingdom of Heaven is like unto a man that is a merchant seeking goodly pearls; and having found one of great price, he went and sold all that he had and bought it."

[2] Exodus xxviii.

[3] Compare the first chapters in Ernest Babelon's Les origines de la monnaie considérés au point de vue économique et historique, Paris, 1897.

"wedge" (in the original "tongue," Joshua vii, 21),[1] disks (*kikkar*), or rings (often represented on Egyptian monuments), which undoubtedly had a fixed valuation and weight. Generally the metal was weighed on scales to determine its value. Thus the name of the piece of money most frequently occurring in the Bible, *shekel*, properly denotes "weight" (from *shaqal*, "to weigh"), and to this day it is usual in the East to examine and test carefully by weight all coins received.

After the exile we find mentioned *adarkon* and *darkemon*,[2] apparently as weights for money, which are usually identified in name with the Persian gold daric. Upon the overthrow of the Persian monarchy Greek coins of the denominations of talents and drachms probably began to circulate in Palestine.

While some attribute the first coinage of the shekel to Ezra, the earliest native Jewish coins known are shekels and half shekels of silver, and one-sixth skekel of bronze, struck by Simon Maccabæus[3] about 146 B. C. The succeeding Maccabæan or Hasmonæan princes down to 37 B. C. struck small bronze coins with Hebrew or Hebrew and Greek inscriptions. The Idumæan or Herodian princes coined bronze money bearing their names in Greek characters. At the same time the Roman procurators of Judæa (from 6 B. C.) also struck coins with Greek inscriptions. The last coins struck by the Jews were those during the revolt under Bar-Cochba (132 A. D.). Greek and Roman money was current in Palestine in addition to the native Hebrew coins, as seen from the New Testament.[4]

Money mentioned in the Bible.

I. HEBREW MONEY.

Talent (*kikkar*).	Mina (*maneh*).	Shekel.	One-half shekel (*beka*).	One-fourth shekel (*reba*).	One-twentieth shekel (*gerah*).	United States currency, about—
1 =	60 =	3,000 =	6,000 =	12,000 =	60,000 =	$1,920.00
	1 =	50 =	100 =	200 =	1,000 =	32.00
		1 =	2 =	4 =	20 =	.64
			1 =	2 =	10 =	.32
				1 =	5 =	.16
					1 =	.03½

II. PERSIAN MONEY.

Gold daric, weighing 130 grains (*adarkon, darkemon*).	Silver daric, about—	United States currency, about—
1 =	10 =	$5.50
	1 =	.52

---

[1] Dr. Schliemann discovered in the second layer of Troy (the modern Hissarlic) six more or less tongue-shaped silver plaques, which are now preserved in the Royal Museum of Berlin and which are assumed to have served as money; compare Dr. A. Götze, Die Trojanischen Silberbarren der Schliemann-Sammlung, in Globus, LXXI, No. 14.

[2] Ezra viii, 27; Nehemiah vii, 72.

[3] I Maccabees xv, 6.

[4] Compare William C. Prime, Money of the Bible, in the Sunday School Times, 1898, Nos. 15, 17.

Money mentioned in the Bible—Continued.

III. GREEK AND ROMAN MONEY.

Stater.	Tetradrachm.	Shekel.	Didrachm.	Drachm ("piece of silver").	United States currency, about—
1 =	1 =	1 =	2 =	4 =	$0.64
			1 =	2 =	.32
				1 =	.16

Denarius ("pence").	Assarion (As, "farthing").	Quadrant ("farthing").	Lepton ("widow's mite").	United States currency, about—
1 =	10 =	40 =	80 =	$0.16
	1 =	4 =	8 =	.01
		1 =	2 =	.00½
			1 =	.00¼

The following specimens were shown as representing the ancient coinage of places mentioned in the Bible:

SHEKEL.—Made of silver and attributed to Simon Maccabaeus (141-136 B. C.), to whom Antiochus VII Sidetes "gave leave to coin money for thy country with thine own stamp."[1] Obverse, a cup representing the pot of manna,[2] with the legend: "Shekel of Israel. Year two;" reverse, the budding rod of Aaron,[3] with the legend: "Jerusalem the Holy." (See plate 9, fig. 1.) The value of the shekel in United States currency was about 64 cents. The average shekel weighs between 200 and 220 grains, Troy weight.

TWO COINS OF JOHN HYRCANUS (136-106 B. C.).—Original of copper. Obverse, "Jochanan, High Priest and Prince of the Jewish Confederation;" reverse, two cornucopias and a poppy head. (See plate 9, fig. 3.)

WIDOW'S MITE.—Coin of Alexander Jannaeus (105-78 B. C.).—Copper (facsimile). Obverse, "Jonathan the High Priest and the Confederation of the Jews," within a wreath of olive; reverse, two cornucopias and a poppy head. (See plate 9, fig. 4.) It is assumed that this or a similar coin is referred to by the term "widow's mite" in Mark xii, 42. It is true that in the original it bears the Greek name *lepton* $\lambda \varepsilon \pi \tau \acute{o} \nu$, Latin *minutum*, but a Jewish coin must be assumed here, none other being permitted within the temple precincts. The mite was the smallest current Jewish coin in the times of Jesus, and was also the smallest temple contribution legally admissible. Its value in the United States currency was about one-eighth of a cent.

COIN OF HEROD ANTIPAS.—Bronze. Obverse (in Greek characters), "Herod Tetrarch," with a palm branch; reverse, "Tiberias," within a wreath. (See plate 9, fig. 6.) Herod Antipas, Tetrarch of Galilee and Peraea, A. D. 4-39, is often mentioned in the New Testament.[4] It was he who beheaded John the Baptist, and to him was Jesus sent for examination, by Pilate.[5] In honor of the Emperor Tiberias he founded the city of Tiberias, on the western shore of the Sea of Gennesareth, where the coin was struck.

---

[1] 1 Maccabees xv, 6.
[2] Exodus xvi, 33.
[3] Numbers xvii, 8.
[4] Matthew xiv, 1-3; Luke iii, 1, 19, etc.
[5] Luke xxiii, 7.

COIN OF HEROD PHILIP II (died A. D. 34).—Struck at Cæsarea Philippi in honor of the Eighth Roman Legion. Copper. Obverse, "Herod Philip," with his portrait; reverse, the standards of the Legion. (See plate 9, fig. 7.) Herod Philip is mentioned [1] as Tetrarch of Iturea; Cæsarea Philippi was often visited by Jesus.[2] It is now a small village called Banijas, near Mount Hermon.

COIN OF AGRIPPA II (last Jewish King).—Bronze. Obverse, name and head of the Emperor; reverse, "Money of Agrippa, struck at Neronias" (Cæsarea Philippi). (See plate 9, fig. 2.) Herod Agrippa II was the last Jewish King, 48-100 A. D.[3]

His long reign was coincident with that of the Roman emperors Claudius, Nero, Galba, Otho, Vitelius, Vespasian, Titus, Domitan, Nerva, Trajan, and his coins are therefore found bearing the effigies of several emperors. He is mentioned [4] as having an interview with the Apostle Paul in the presence of the Roman Governor Festus at Cæsarea.

DENARIUS, OR ROMAN TRIBUTE PENNY.—Silver (two specimens). Obverse, "Tiberius Cæsar," son of deified Agustus (Emperor 14-37 A. D.); reverse, "Pontifex Maximus" (Chief Priest). It contained 60 grains Troy of silver, and its value was about 16 cents. (See plate 9, fig. 12.) The denarius was the tribute money that the Jews had to pay to the Romans, and it is very likely that a variety of this coin was shown Jesus with the question "Is it lawful to give tribute unto Cæsar or not?"[5] The denarius seems to have been the ordinary day's wages of the Palestinian peasantry.[6] It is mentioned eleven times in the Gospels [7] and once in the Revelation (vi, 6). The translation in the English versions, penny, is misleading.

STATER.—Antioch. Silver (facsimile, two specimens). Obverse, "(Money) of Cæsar Augustus" (first Roman Emperor, 29 B. C. to 14 A. D.), with head of the Emperor; reverse, Tyche, as genius of the city of Antioch, with her foot on the river god Orontes, and the words, "Thirtieth year of the victory" (i. e., Actium). (See plate 9, fig. 5.) The stater, about equal in value to the shekel, is mentioned (Revised Version, "shekel"; margin, "stater") as the coin which would be found by Peter in the mouth of the fish, sufficient to pay the Temple tribute, which was half a shekel, for Jesus and himself.[8]

COIN OF CÆSAREA.—Bronze. Obverse, head of Agustus Cæsar. (See plate 9, fig. 8.) Cæsarea, founded by Herod I, is frequently mentioned in the Acts. It was the scene of the conversion of the centurion

---

[1] Luke iii, 1.
[2] Matthew xvi, 13; Mark viii, 27.
[3] Graetz, History of the Jews, pp. 50-93.
[4] Acts xxvi, 2, 28.
[5] Matthew xxii, 17.
[6] Idem, xx, 2.
[7] Idem, xviii, 28; xx, 2, 9, 10, 13; xxii, 17; Mark vi, 37; xii, 15; xiv, 5; Luke vii, 41; x, 35; xx, 24; John vi, 7; xii, 5.
[8] Idem, xvii, 27.

Cornelius (x); Philip preached the Gospel here (xxi, 8); Paul was imprisoned here two years before he was sent to Rome (xxiv–xxvi). It was the residence of the Roman governors, and here the Jewish war against Rome broke out.

TETRADRACHM OF SIDON.—Silver. Obverse, head of the city; reverse, "(Money of the Sidonians) Holy and inviolable," with the figure of Astarte. (See plate 9, fig. 9.) The value of a tetradrachm was about the same as of the shekel, or 64 cents. Sidon, the oldest city of Phenicia, is often mentioned in the Bible. It is at present represented by the town of Saida, with about 15,000 inhabitants.

TETRADRACHMS OF TYRE.—Silver. Obverse; Head of Hercules as Baal (Lord) of the city. (See plate 9, figs. 13, 14.) Tyre, next to Sidon the oldest and most important city of Phenicia, is often referred to in the Bible. During the period of David and Solomon friendly relations were entertained between Tyre and Israel.[1] The coast of Tyre was visited by Jesus,[2] and Paul landed at Tyre on one of his missionary voyages.[3] The modern Çur is an unimportant town, with about 5,000 inhabitants.

COIN OF ASHKELON.—Bronze. Struck by order of Emperor Alexander Severus, about A. D. 228. (See plate 9, figs. 11.)

Ascalon, or Ashkelon, was one of the five cities of the Philistines, 30 miles southwest of Jerusalem;[4] it was the center of the worship of Derceto, the supposed female counterpart of Dagon. It is now represented by the village of Askalan.

COINS OF THE CITY OF DAMASCUS.—Copper (two specimens). (See plate 9, fig. 10.) Damascus, the ancient capital of Syria, is mentioned as early as in the times of Abraham.[5] Later, it frequently came in contact with Israel.[6] In the New Testament it is especially known from the history of the Apostle Paul.[7]

TETRADRACHM OF THE CITY OF BABYLON.—Silver. Struck by Mazaios, governor under Alexander the Great, 331–328 B. C. (See plate 9, fig. 16.)

TETRADRACHM OF ALEXANDER THE GREAT (336–323 B. C.).—Silver. Obverse, head of the king; reverse, Zeus (Jupiter) seated holding the eagle. (See plate 9, fig. 15.)

Alexander, King of Macedonia and the famous conqueror, is mentioned by name in I Maccabees vi, 2. It is also assumed that he is typified under the emblem of the "he-goat" in Daniel viii, 5, and that his empire is meant by the "fourth monarchy" depicted in Daniel ii, 40 and vii, 7, 23f.

TETRADRACHM OF SELEUCUS I NICATOR, KING OF SYRIA, 312–280 B. C.—Silver. Obverse, head of Seleucus; reverse, figure of Jupiter.

---

[1] I Kings, v.
[2] Matthew xv, 21; Mark vii, 24.
[3] Acts xxi, 3.
[4] Joshua xiii, 3; 1 Samuel vi, 17.
[5] Genesis xiv, 15; xv, 2.
[6] II Samuel viii, 6; II Kings xvi, 9, etc.
[7] Acts ix; xxii, 6.

(See plate 9, fig. 17.) The city of Seleucia, the principal port of Antioch, from which Paul and Barnabas set out for Cyprus,[1] was named after Seleucus I.

COIN OF DEMETRIUS SOTER.—Obverse, head of Demetrius; reverse, "King Demetrius Soter," with seated female figure. (See plate 9, fig. 19.) Demetrius Soter, King of Syria 162-150 B. C., waged war against the Maccabees and is often mentioned in the books of the Maccabees.[2]

STATER OF TARSUS.—Silver. 380-360 B. C. Obverse, Baal enthroned within a circle of turrets; reverse, Satrap Tarcamos seated, holding one arrow. (See plate 9, fig. 18.) Tarsus, the ancient capital of Cilicia, Asia Minor, was the home of the Apostle Paul.[3] It is still a city of about 10,000 inhabitants. It is now accessible from Alexandretta by rail.

COIN OF CYPRUS.—Bronze. Struck under Emperor Claudius (A. D. 41-54) and the Proconsul Sergius Paulus. (See plate 9, fig. 20.) Cyprus, one of the largest islands in the Mediterranean, was the birthplace of Barnabas,[4] and often visited by Paul while Sergius was its proconsul.[5] In the Old Testament it is referred to by the name of Kittim, which name is, however, also used in some passages in a wider sense for the Greek coasts and islands of the Mediterranean.

TETRADRACHMS OF EPHESUS.—Silver. Struck 140 B. C. (two specimens). (See plate 9, fig. 25.) Ephesus, in ancient time one of the most important cities in Asia Minor, was especially celebrated for its Temple of Diana.[6] It was the place of residence of Paul,[7] of Timothy,[8] and of the Apostle John, who probably died there. Ephesus was one of the seven churches referred to in the Apocalypse.[9] It was also the seat of the third General Council (A. D. 431) and of the "Robber Synod" (A. D. 449). Numerous ruins are still to be seen there.

HEMIDRACHMS OF EPHESUS.—Silver. Struck 200 B. C. Obverse, Bee; reverse, Deer (two specimens). (See plate 9, fig. 26.)

AES (= AS) OF THESSALONICA).—Copper. Struck 88 B. C. Obverse, head of Janus; reverse, Dioscuri. (See plate 9, fig. 21.) The *as* or *assarius*, in the Greek New Testament ἀσσάριον (assarion), in the English version "farthing," was the original Roman coin, and was at one time the unit in Roman numeration both of weight and currency. The Greeks adopted the name of the coin and used it upon their autonomous coins. The *as* of the New Testament was of the value of one-sixteenth of a denarius and nearly the size of an English halfpenny. It is mentioned in Matthew x, 29 and 30: "Are not two sparrows sold for a farthing, and one of them shall not fall on the ground

---

[1] Acts xiii, 4.
[2] I Maccabees viii, 31; x, 1, etc.
[3] Acts ix, 11, 30; xi, 25; xxii, 3.
[4] Idem, iv, 36.
[5] Idem, xiii, 4.
[6] Acts xix, 35.
[8] Idem, xix.
[7] I Timothy i, 3.
[9] Apocalypse ii, 4.

without your Father; but the very hairs of your head are all numbered."[1] In Matthew v, 26, the last "farthing" is referred to, and in Mark xii, 42, we read "two mites, which make a farthing." The Greek word is κοδράντης (*Kodrantes*, Latin *quadrans*), which was one-fourth of an *as*. Thessalonica, formerly the capital of Macedonia, where the coin was struck, is the modern Salonica. Two Epistles of Paul are addressed to the Christians of this place.

COIN OF THESSALONICA.—Copper. Struck 158 B. C. Obverse, head of City of Nymph; reverse, Galley. (See plate 9, fig. 22.)

TETRADRACHM OF MACEDONIA.—Silver. Struck between 156 and 146 B. C. Obverse, head of Minerva upon a Macedonian shield; reverse, Club of Hercules. (See plate 9, fig. 27.) Macedonia is often mentioned in the New Testament. Paul visited this province on his second and third missionary voyages and founded congregations in several of its cities.[2]

DIDRACHMS OF ATHENS.—Silver (two specimens) (470 to 230 B. C.). Obverse, head of Athene (Minerva); reverse, Owl. (See plate 9, fig. 24.) Athens, the former capital of Attica and the modern capital of Greece, was visited by Paul, where he delivered the discourse on the Areopagus.[3]

TETRADRACHMS OF ATHENS.—Silver (470 to 230 B. C.). Obverse, head of Athene (Minerva); reverse, Owl (the bird sacred to Athene) (two specimens). (See plate 9, fig. 23.)

CHILD'S BANK.—Pottery. Excavated at Ostia (seaport of ancient Rome), 1886, by Dr. Thomas Wilson. (See plate 9, fig. 28.)

When found the bank consisted of a single piece of pottery. In the top was a slit through which the money was dropped. It contained 145 silver coins of the Roman Consular or Familia series. As these coins were issued from 200 to 19 B. C., and none of a later date were in the find, it is to be presumed that the bank was buried a short time before the Christian era. The silver denarii in the bank are part of the original lot found with the bank.

DRESS, ORNAMENTS, AND HOUSEHOLD UTENSILS.

The fashion of dress and ornament, as well as the form of household utensils, are, it may be assumed, in the "unchanging East" essentially the same at the present day as in Bible times, and the collection shown of objects of modern life and industry in the Orient explain or illustrate many allusions in the Scriptures.

The objects were as follows:

SHEEPSKIN COAT. (See plate 10.) Skins of animals were the primitive material used for clothing,[4] and pelisses of sheepskin still form an ordinary article of dress in the East. The mantle of the

---

[1] Luke xii, 6.
[2] Acts xvi and xx.
[3] Acts xvii, 15ff.
[4] Genesis iii, 21.

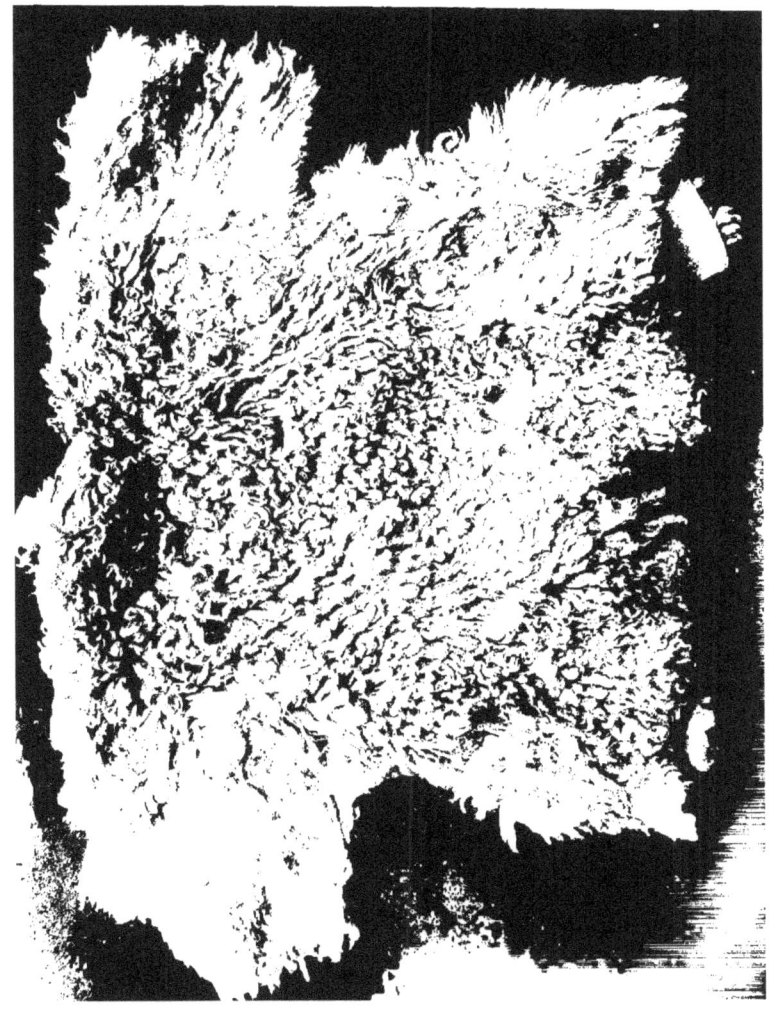

Prophet Elijah[1] was probably the skin of a sheep or some animal with the hair left on, wherefore he is called the "hairy man."[2] It was characteristic of the prophet's office.[3] "Beware of false prophets, which come to you in sheep's clothing, but inwardly are ravening wolves." "And it shall come to pass in that day that the prophets shall be ashamed every one of his vision when he prophesieth; neither shall they wear a hairy mantle to deceive." "The prophet's (Elijah's) dress proclaimed the mountaineer of the Arabian border exactly the same as is worn to-day; the undergarment bound with a broad leather belt, and over it a loose, coarse cloak of sheepskin, with the wool outside, its dark-brown folds floating in the wind as he hurriedly strode along with beard bare and long black locks covering his neck, for he was a Nazarite. The Moslem prophet-dervish, as different from the *mollah* or dervish of the towns as Elijah from a Levite of Jerusalem, exactly copies this dress and habit."[4]

MALE COSTUME OF BAGDAD, MESOPOTAMIA.—The general characteristics of Oriental dress have been much the same in all ages. The representations on monuments correspond in general to the raiment in present use. They are the same loose, flowing robes, which can easily be adapted to various purposes. The garments mentioned in the Bible as generally used are the *Ketoneth* (Greek, $\chi\iota\tau\acute{\omega}\nu$, *chiton;* English versions, "coat"), a kind of shirt worn next to the skin, corresponding to the modern *qamis*. It reached to the knees or ankles and was either sleeveless or provided only with short sleeves. A person wearing the *Ketoneth* alone is described as naked.[5] Over the shirt there was worn during the day the *me'îl* (English versions, "cloak"), which had loose sleeves and was longer than the shirt, answering to the modern *Kaftan*. It was thrown off when the wearer engaged in manual labor. It was fastened by a girdle and the folds thus formed were used as pockets. It was and is sometimes woven in one piece.[6] These garments are referred to by Jesus in Matthew v, 40: "And if any man would go to law with thee and take away thy coat (Greek $\chi\iota\tau\acute{\omega}\nu$, *chiton*), let him have thy cloak (ἱμάτιον, *himation*) also." Over these was worn an outer garment, referred to by the terms *simlah*, *beged*, *kesuth*, and *lebush*. It consisted of a rectangular piece of woolen cloth, something like a Scotch plaid, and answered to the modern *lungi* in Central Asia or the *ab'eih* in Egypt, and varied in size and quality with the means of the wearer. There is no special allusion to headdress (except as an ornamental appendage in the description of the dress of the priests). The ordinary headdress of the Bedouin consists of the *Kuffiyeh*, a square handkerchief, generally of red and yellow cotton, or cotton and silk,

---

[1] I Kings xix, 13, 19; II Kings ii, 13.
[2] II Kings i, 8.
[3] Matthew vii, 15; Zechariah xiii, 4.
[4] H. B. Tristram, Eastern Customs in Bible Lands, p. 166.
[5] I Samuel xix, 24; Isaiah xx, 2; John, xxi, 7.
[6] John xix, 23. Compare Tristram, Eastern Customs in Bible Lands, p. 156.

folded so that three of the corners hang down over the neck and shoulders, leaving the face exposed, and bound round the head by a cord, and it is probable that in ancient time the head was protected in a similar manner. For the protection of the feet sandals were worn, consisting of leather soles fastened to the foot by means of thongs. Shoes seem to have been worn by women for ornamental purposes.[1]

WOMAN'S COSTUME OF BAGDAD, MESOPOTAMIA.—The costume of women was essentially similar to that of men. There was sufficient difference, however, to mark the sex, and it was strictly forbidden to a woman to wear "that which pertaineth unto a man" and to a man "to put on a woman's garment" *simlah*.[2] The difference, probably, consisted chiefly in the outer garment. That of woman is called *Mitpahath*,[3] *ma'atâfâh*,[4] both designating a kind of wrapper or shawl. There are mentioned besides *ça'if*,[5] probably a garment of light, gauzy material, *radid*,[6] a similar robe, *pethigil*,[7] explained to denote a wrap of some sort or a girdle.

SYRIAN COAT.—Called in Syriac *Abba*. It consists of red cloth embroidered in white and is worn as an outer garment.

SILVER NECKLACE (Hebrew, *Ănaq*). (See plate 11, fig. 1.) Necklaces, like many other ornaments, were worn by both sexes.[8] They consisted of a single band or chain, or of a series of ornaments, as pearls or pieces of corals, strung together.[9] The custom of wearing a necklace is figuratively referred to in Proverbs i, 9: "For they shall be a chaplet of grace unto thy head and chains about thy neck." Animals ridden by kings were decorated with collars of precious metals,[10] and it is still the custom in the East to decorate riding beasts in this way.

SILVER ANKLETS (Hebrew, *Ăkasîm*). (See plate 11, fig. 4.) Anklets worn by women as ornaments are mentioned in Isaiah iii, 16, 18. From these passages it would seem that the tinkling produced by knocking the anklets against each other was their chief attraction. To increase the sound, pebbles were sometimes inclosed in them. They were also worn by the ancient Egyptians, Greeks, and Romans, and are still general in India and in Africa. They were sometimes connected by the "anklet chains"[11] (Hebrew, *Ce'adah*), which compelled those who wore them to take short, mincing steps.

GOLD NOSE RING (Hebrew, *Nezem*). (See plate 11, fig. 3.) The Hebrew

---

[1] Ezekiel xvi, 10; Canticles vii, 2. Compare Judith x, 4; xvi, 9.
[2] Deuteronomy xxii, 5.
[3] Ruth iii, 15; Isaiah iii, 22.
[4] Isaiah iii, 22; English versions, "mantle, shawl."
[5] Genesis xxiv, 65; English versions, "veil."
[6] Isaiah iii, 23; Canticles v, 7.
[7] *Idem*, iii, 24.
[8] Genesis xli, 42; Daniel v, 29.
[9] Canticles i, 10; iv, 9.
[10] Judges viii, 26.
[11] They are referred to in Isaiah iii, 20.

EXPLANATION OF PLATE 11.

```
                    6
            4    7
        2            9
    1   3   5
                8
```

Fig. 1. NECKLACE (*anaq*).
(Cat. No. 151727, U. S. N. M. Bagdad, Turkey. Collected by Rev. Dr. John P. Peters.)

Fig. 2. JEWISH WEDDING RING.
(Cat. No. 154435, U. S. N. M. Philadelphia, Pa. Deposited by Mayer Sulzberger.)

Fig. 3. NOSE RING (*nezem*).
(Cat. No. 151728, U. S. N. M. Bagdad, Turkey. Collected by Rev. Dr. John P. Peters.)

Figs. 4, 5. ANKLETS (*akasim*).
(Cat. No. 151726, U. S. N. M. Bagdad, Turkey. Collected by Rev. Dr. John P. Peters.)

Figs. 6–8. KOHL.
(Cat. No. 151729, U. S. N. M. Bagdad, Turkey. Collected by Rev. Dr. John P. Peters.)
IMPLEMENTS FOR PAINTING THE EYES.
(Cat. Nos. 74562, 74563, U. S. N. M. Egypt. Collected by George W. Samson.)

Fig. 9. SYRIAN INKHORN.
(Cat. No. 74618, U. S. N. M. Palestine. Collected by George W. Samson.)

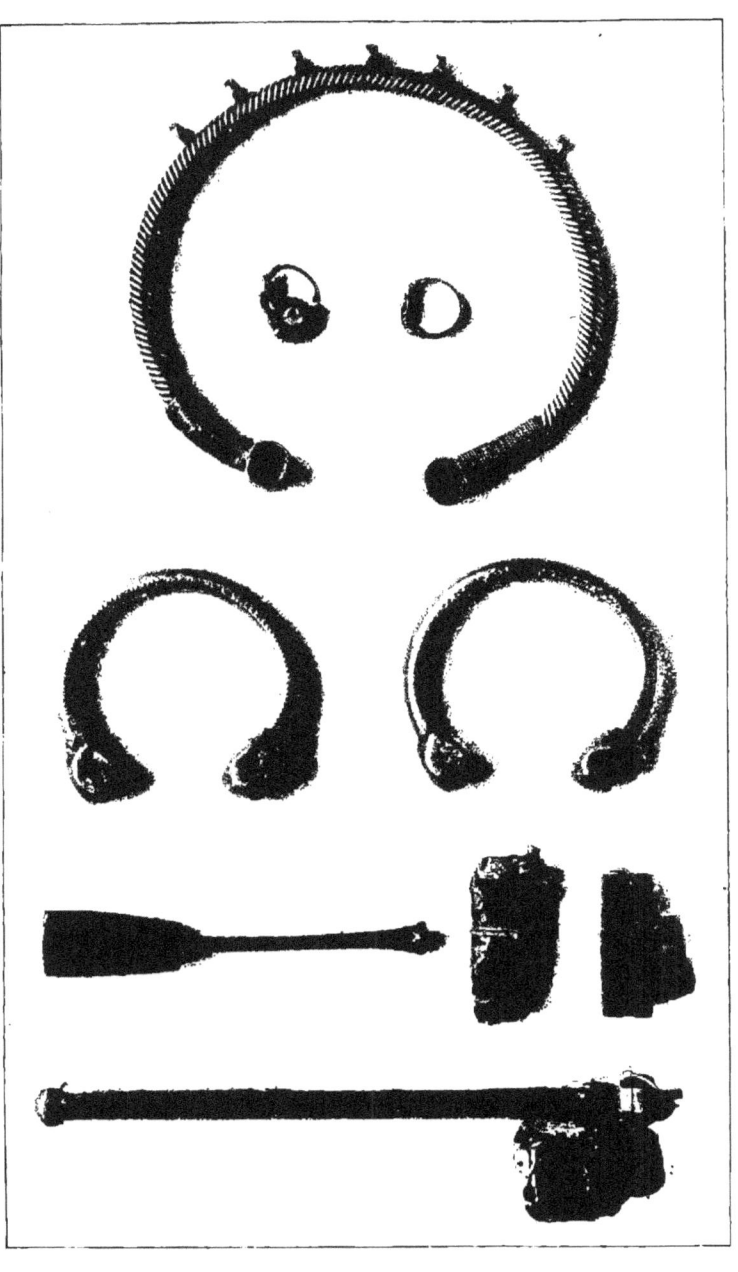

EASTERN ORNAMENTS.

word *nezem* denotes both an earring and a nose ring.[1] In modern times the rings are often of extraordinary size and frequently reach to the mouth, so that they must be removed in eating. Sometimes the nose and ears are connected by a series of rings interlinked with one another.

KOHL AND ANCIENT AND MODERN IMPLEMENTS USED IN PAINTING THE EYES (Hebrew, *Puch;* Aramean, *Kuhala*). (See plate 11, figs. 6, 8.) The practice of applying pigments to the eyelids and eyebrows in order to enhance the brilliancy of the eyes was common in Bible times,[2] and is still in everyday practice in the East. The pigment, which is a preparation of antimony, is applied to the eyelids by means of a small blunt piece of wood or ivory, which is moistened, dipped in the mixture, and then drawn carefully along the edges of the eye. From the Arabic name kohl comes the term "alcohol," the fineness of the powder suggesting the idea of highly rectified spirits.

MILLSTONES (Hebrew, *Rehaim*) (see plate 12, figs. 1, 2), and a modern photograph showing women grinding corn. (See plate 13.) Millstones are often referred to in the Bible, and they are still used in grinding corn in the same form as in ancient times. They consist of two cylindrical stones. The lower one is firmly planted on the ground and provided with a convex upper surface, on which the concave under surface of the other stone revolves. The upper stone, which is called *rekeb* or "rider," has a hole through its center, into which the grain is dropped, and through which runs a shaft to hold the stone in place. A handle attached to the "rider" enables a person sitting near to turn it around and grind the grain, which is fed with the hand that is free.

Layard[3] describes the grinding of corn by the modern Arabs as follows: "The wandering Arabs have no other means of grinding their corn than by hand mills, which they carry with them wherever they go. They are always worked by the women, for it is considered unworthy of a man to engage in any domestic occupation. * * * The grain is passed through the hole of the pivot, and the flour is collected in a cloth spread under the mill. It is then mixed with water, kneaded in a wooden bowl, and pressed by the hand into round balls ready for baking. During these processes the women are usually seated on the ground. Hence in Isaiah xlvii, 1, 2, the daughter of Babylon is told to sit in the dust and on the ground and "to take the millstones to grind meal." It was forbidden to take the mill or even the upper stone in pledge, as taking "the life" (that is the means of sustaining life).[4] As each day so much grain was ground as was needed, the "voice of the mill" became proverbial.[5]

---

[1] Genesis xxiv, 47; Isaiah iii, 21, and Proverbs xi, 32.

[2] Jeremiah iv, 30: "Though thou enlargest thine eyes with paint, in vain dost thou make thyself fair: thy lovers despise thee, they seek thy life." (Compare Ezekiel xxiii, 40; Proverbs vi, 25.)

[3] Layard, Nineveh and Babylon, abridged edition, p. 127.

[4] Deuteronomy xxiv, 6.

[5] Jeremiah xxv, 10.

GOATSKIN WATERBAG (Hebrew, *Nod* and *Hemeth*). (See plate 12, fig. 3.) Skin bottles were commonly used.[1] Jesus employs them in a comparison: "Neither do men put new wine into old wine-skins" (margin, "skins used as bottles").[2] Such bottles are made from the whole skins of animals, generally the goat. After the animal is killed and its feet and head removed the rest of the body is drawn out entire without opening the belly, and after the skin has been tanned the places where the legs were cut off are sewn up and when filled it is tied about the neck. These skin bottles were also used to contain milk, and in them the milk was churned. To the corners of the skin bottle filled with milk cords are tied and the skin is thus suspended from three sticks, which are inclined so as to meet at a point above. A girl sits beneath and moves the suspended bottle to and fro.[3] Skin bottles are also in use in Spain, in the City of Mexico, and by the Eskimos.

BIRD TRAP (Hebrew, *Pah*). (See plate 14, fig. 1.) The most usual method of catching birds was by the trap, which consisted of two parts, a net strained over a frame and a stick or spring (Hebrew *mogesh*) to support it, but so placed that it should give way to the slightest touch. The bird trap is frequently used in comparisons for the ensnaring of the heedless and the weak.[4] "Can a bird fall in a snare upon the earth where no gin is set for him? Shall a snare spring up from the ground and have taken nothing at all?" "Our soul is escaped as a bird out of the snare of the fowlers." "He goeth after her straightway * * * as a bird hasteth to the snare, and knoweth not that it is for his life." "A gin shall take him by the heel and a snare shall lay hold on him." "As the birds that are caught in the snare, even so are the sons of men snared in an evil time, when it falleth suddenly upon them."

SLING (Hebrew, *Qela'*). (See plate 14, fig. 2.) The sling as a weapon of war is first mentioned in the Book of Judges (xx, 16). David killed Goliath with a stone thrown from a sling.[5] The Israelitish army was provided with companies of slingers.[6] The sling was also employed in the wars of the Roman against the Jews.[7] According to the monuments the sling was both an Egyptian and an Assyrian weapon. It consisted of a strip of leather or woven material, wide in the middle to receive the missile, and narrowing at both ends into a rope. Not only were smooth stones used for hurling, but balls made of burnt clay, of lead, and various other hard substances. It is still used by shepherds to drive away wild animals from their herds as in the time of David.

---

[1] Genesis xxi, 14; Joshua ix, 5.
[2] Matthew ix, 17.
[3] Picturesque Palestine, p. 48.
[4] Amos iii, 5; Psalms cxxiv, 7; Proverbs vii, 23; Job xviii, 9; Ecclesiastes ix, 12.
[5] I Samuel xvii, 40.
[6] II Kings iii, 25.
[7] Josephus, Wars of the Jews, ii, 7, 18; iv, 1, 3.

EXPLANATION OF PLATE 12.

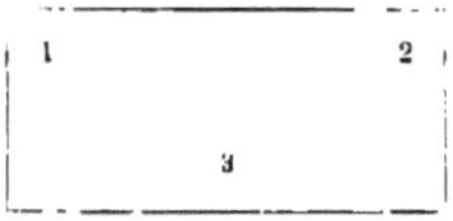

Figs. 1, 2. MILLSTONES.
(Cat. No. 151827, U. S. N. M. Bagdad, Turkey. Collected by Rev. Dr. John P. Peters.)

Fig. 3. GOATSKIN WATERBAG.
(Cat. No. 74627, U. S. N. M. Palestine. Collected by George W. Samson.)

MILLSTONES AND GOATSKIN WATERBAG.

WOMEN GRINDING CORN BY HAND MILL.
Cat. No. 151405, U.S.N.M.

EXPLANATION OF PLATE 14.

Fig. 1. BIRD TRAP (*pah*).
  (Cat. No. 151842, U. S. N. M. Bagdad, Turkey. Collected by Rev. Dr. John P. Peters.)
Fig. 2. SLING (*qela*).
  (Cat. No. 166249, U. S. N. M. Damascus, Syria. Collected by Dr. G. Brown Goode.)
Figs. 3, 4. DOOR LOCK AND KEY.
  (Cat. No. 151840. U. S. N. M. Bagdad, Turkey. Collected by Rev. Dr. John P. Peters.)

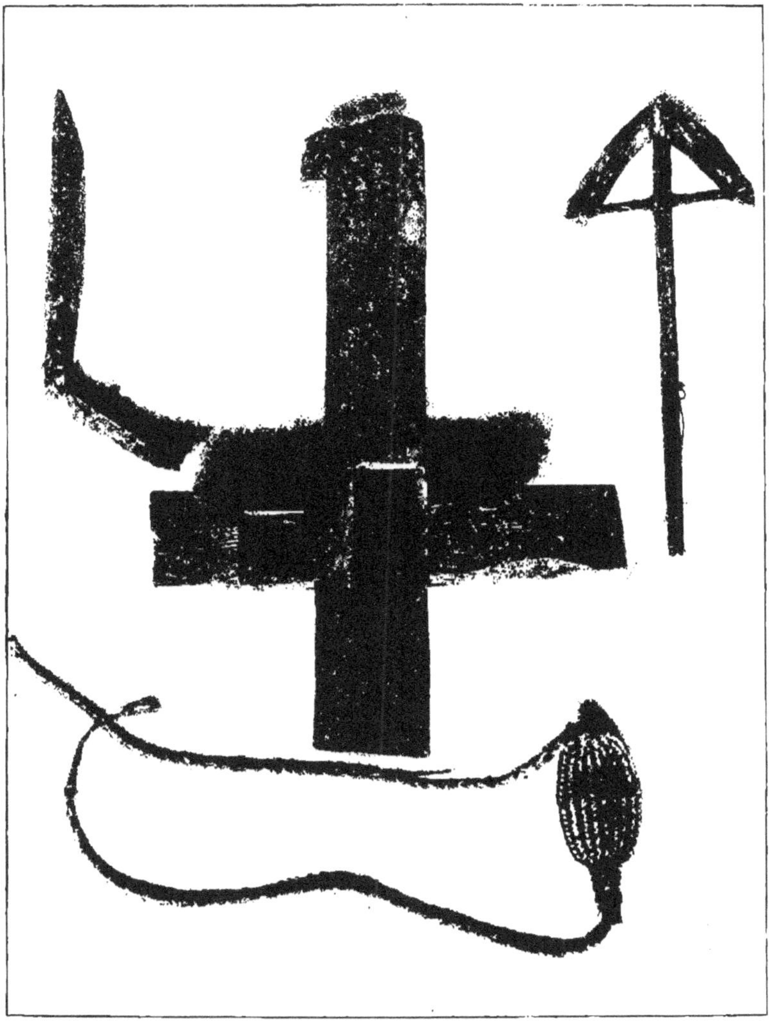

BIRD TRAP, SLING, AND DOOR LOCK.

WOODEN DOOR LOCK AND KEY. (See plate 14, fig. 3.) The doors of Eastern houses, which are usually small and low, seem early to have been provided with hinges turning in sockets, and with locks and keys,[1] in whose construction no little ingenuity was displayed. Formerly, as now, it is likely that locks and keys were made both of iron and of wood, according to circumstances. The wooden key now quite generally in use consists of a piece of wood about a foot in length provided at one end with a series of pegs. It is thrust into a little opening at the side of the door and applied to the bolt. This has a corresponding series of holes into which the pegs of the key fit, displacing thereby another set of pegs by which the bolt is held in its place.[2]

SYRIAN INKHORN (Hebrew, *Qeseth ha sofer*). (See plate 11, fig. 9.) The most common writing material among the Hebrews was probably papyrus or dressed skins. This at least must have been the case in the time of Jeremiah, as the expression "roll of a book"[3] points to some pliant material. Ink (Hebrew, *deyo*), which was made of soot, is mentioned in Jeremiah xxxvi, 18. The pen used for writing on papyrus or parchment was no doubt the reed pen still common in the Orient and until recently in southern Europe.[4] The inkhorn is mentioned in Ezekiel ix, 2, as being carried "by the side;" that is, fastened to the girdle of the scribe. It is still carried in this fashion in the Orient. The inkhorn consists of a tube containing reed pens and a receptacle for ink.

JEWISH RELIGIOUS CEREMONIAL.

The next collection was one of objects of Jewish religious ceremonial, which had their origin in and are based upon Biblical ordinances. The following specimens were shown:

MANUSCRIPT COPY OF THE PENTATEUCH, OR FIVE BOOKS OF MOSES IN HEBREW, *Sefer Torah.*—The Pentateuch or law (Hebrew, *Torah*) is considered by the Jews the most important part of the Bible. A section of it is read every Sabbath in the synagogue in the morning service, and shorter portions in the afternoon service, on holidays, fasts, and on Monday and Thursday mornings of every week. This latter usage goes back to the days of the early synagogue when Monday and Thursday were court and market days, and the peasants coming to town to dispose of their produce would attend worship. A manuscript copy is employed, printed copies not being used. When not in use the roll is covered with a cloak and placed upright in an ark or chest.

POINTER (Hebrew, *Yad*, properly "hand").—The pointer is used in the service of the synagogue during the reading of the law to prevent

---

[1] Judges iii, 23, 25; Canticles v, 5; Nehemiah iii, 3.
[2] Bissel, Biblical Antiquities, p. 23.
[3] Jeremiah xxxvi, 2.
[4] Compare Jeremiah viii, 8; Psalms xlv, 2; III John, 13.

the reader from losing the place. It is usually made in the shape of a hand, hence its Hebrew name.

SILVER BREASTPLATE OF THE TORAH.—On the top are the two tablets engraved with the Ten Commandments, surmounted by the "crown of the law" upheld by two lions, the symbol of the tribe of Judah. Inside the tablets are engraved, on a sliding plate, the names of the various festivals. (See plate 15.) The manuscript copy of the Pentateuch, or the *Sefer Torah*, being the most precious object used in Jewish ceremonies, is, when not in use, covered with a mantle of costly material, sometimes adorned with a breastplate, bells, or crown, and put upright in the "holy ark" (*aron ha-kodesh*).

VEIL OF THE HOLY ARK (*Parocheth*).—Made in Constantinople, Turkey. (See plate 16.) The border of green velvet is embroidered in gold and silver with flowers. The center, of red velvet, has in the four corners, in Hebrew, the names of the four archangels, Raphael, Gabriel, Uriel, and Michael. On the top are the words, "But the Lord is in His holy temple; let all the earth keep silence before Him,"[1] and "I have set the Lord always before me."[2] Below is a burning lamp hanging down by chains, symbolizing the light which emanates from the law of God. On the sides are the words, "This is the gate of the Lord; the righteous shall enter into it."[3] In the Holy Ark (*aron ha-kodesh*) are kept the scrolls of the law, or the Pentateuch, written on parchment, for use in the service of the synagogue. The "Holy Ark" is, therefore, the most important part of the synagogue, and is richly adorned. Whenever it is opened the congregation rises in reverence for the Law of God it contains.

SABBATH LAMP.—Used by the German Jews in their houses. It was manufactured in the eighteenth century in Fellheim, Germany. (See plate 17, fig. 1.) The celebration of the Sabbath is ushered in on its eve (Friday evening) by the housewife lighting candles, reciting the words, "Blessed art Thou, Lord, our God, King of the World, who hath commanded us to light the light of the Sabbath." After that no fire may be handled until the following evening.

KIDDUSH CLOTH.—Silk. Containing in beadwork the tablets of the decalogue in Hebrew, supported by lions. Above are the words, "Remember the Sabbath day, to keep it holy."[4] Before the principal meals of the Sabbath and other feast days the Jews have a special service, including prayers over the wine and bread, which is known as Kiddush, or "sanctification." The head of the family has in front of him a plate containing two loaves of bread, covered by a cloth. The practice of saying a blessing before eating is referred to in I Samuel ix, 13. It no doubt had its origin in the fact that a public meal of any sort was usually preceded by a sacrifice. "Asking the blessing" was

---

[1] Habakkuk ii, 20.
[2] Psalms xvi, 8.
[3] Psalms cxvii, 20.
[4] Exodus xx, 8.

BREASTPLATE OF THE TORAH.
Constantinople.
Cat. No. 154990, U.S.N.M.

VEIL OF THE HOLY ARK (*Parocheth*).
Constantinople.
Cat. No. 154758, U.S.N.M. Collected by Dr. Cyrus Adler.

EXPLANATION OF PLATE 17.

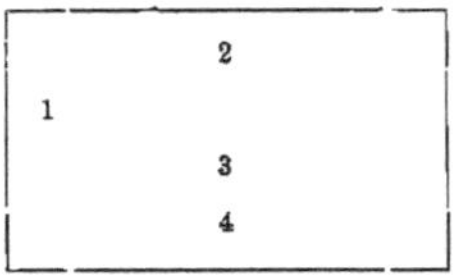

	2
1	3
	4

Fig. 1. SABBATH LAMP.
(Cat. No. 130294, U. S. N. M. Germany.)
Fig. 2. HANUKKAH LAMP.
(Cat. No. 130295, U. S. N. M. Germany.)
Figs. 3, 4. SLAUGHTERING KNIFE AND SCABBARD.
(Cat. No. 154619, U. S. N. M. Germany.)

LAMPS AND SLAUGHTERING KNIFE. GERMANY.

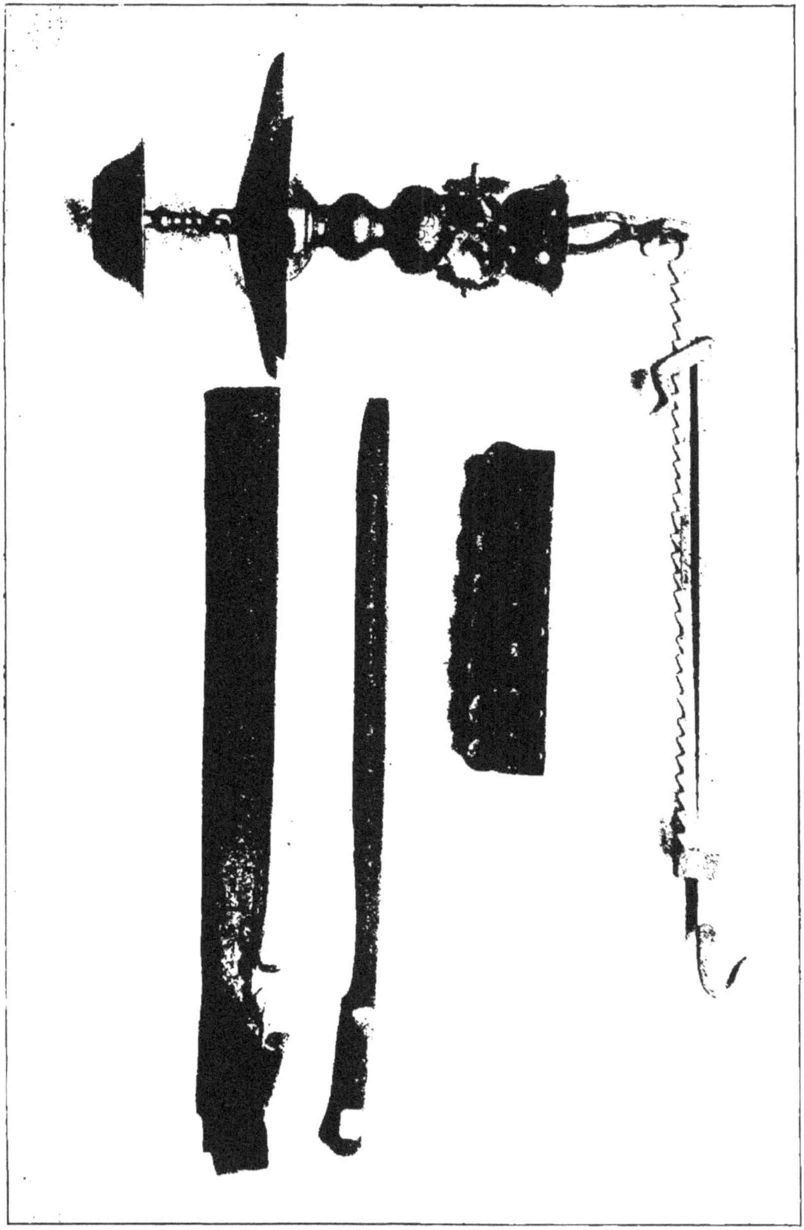

common in New Testament times. The later Jews enjoined also that thanks should be returned after the repast.

SILVER SPICE BOX.—Supposed to have been manufactured in Laupheim (Würtemberg), Germany, about 1740. (See plate 18, fig. 4.) This box, filled with spices, is used in the Jewish service known as *Habdalah* (or separation), the service of the conclusion of the Sabbath. There is a tradition that at the beginning of the Sabbath a special angel accompanies the worshiper from the synagogue; this angel remains with him until the conclusion of the Sabbath. The departure of the angel leaves the man faint, and the spices are intended to restore him. The objects used in this service are a cup of wine, the spice box, and a candle. First a blessing is said over the wine, next over the spices, and last over the light. The cup of wine and the spice box are passed around among the members of the household. The candle is then extinguished by having wine poured upon it.

BRASS PLATE, USED AT THE PASSOVER MEAL.—Adorned with animal figures and flowers and containing an Arabic inscription in Hebrew characters. Made in Constantinople (see plate 19). At the Passover meal (*Seder*, properly "order") a large plate is put on the table, which forms, as it were, the altar of the service. On it are placed the various emblematic articles of the ceremony. These are: a piece of roasted meat, usually the bone of a lamb, representing the Passover lamb; a roasted egg, in memory of the festal sacrifice offered in the Temple; bitter herbs (*maror*, usually horse-radish), in commemoration of the "embittering of life" which Israel suffered in Egyptian servitude;[1] *charoseth*, a compound of almonds, apples, and sirup, which has the color of brick-clay, and into which the bitter herbs are dipped before it is partaken of; some green herbs (lettuce or something similar), as the "food of poverty;" and the unleavened bread or *maççoth*, the principal food of the Passover feast, which is the "bread of affliction, for thou camest forth out of the land of Egypt in haste."[2]

OMER TABLET (manuscript). (See plate 20.) Used in the Synagogue for reckoning the period between Passover and Pentecost. The tablet is in Hebrew. It contains the words, "Blessed art thou, O Lord our God, King of the Universe, who has sanctified us with His Commandments and commanded us to count the Omer." Then follows the count (in Hebrew), and below it the words, "May the Lord restore the worship of the temple speedily in our days," and Psalm lxvii. The letters H, S, and D on the left, mean, respectively, Omer (written Homer by the Spanish Jews), week (Sabbath), and day. The figures on the right indicate that it is the forty-seventh day of Omer, i. e., six weeks and five days. The harvest season was formally opened with the ceremony of waving a sheaf of barley in the sanctuary on the second day of the Passover feast, which began on the 15th of Nisan (March-April).

---

[1] Exodus i, 14.   [2] Deuteronomy xvi, 3.

Before this ceremony took place the harvesting of grain was forbidden:[1] "And ye shall eat neither bread, nor parched corn, nor fresh ears, until this selfsame day, until ye have brought the oblation of your God." From that day seven weeks, or forty-nine days, were counted,[2] to the feast of Pentecost; hence its Hebrew name *Hag ha-Shabuoth* "feast of weeks," and the usual English name "Pentecost," which is the πεντηκοστη *pentekoste*, meaning the fiftieth day. It is also called "feast of harvest,"[3] because the grain harvest then approached its close, and "day of first fruits,"[4] because two loaves of bread from the new wheat were offered on that feast.[5] With the destruction of the Temple the ceremony of waving the sheaf in the Sanctuary necessarily fell away, but the counting is still observed and the prayers contained in the tablet form part of the ritual during the time from Passover to Pentecost.

LULAB AND ETHROG.—The Lulab and Ethrog, bound up with myrtle and willow branches, are used by the Jews at the feast of Tabernacles, in pursuance of the command in Leviticus xxiii, 40: "And ye shall take you on the first day, the fruit of goodly trees, branches of palm trees, and boughs of thick trees and willows of the brook, and ye shall rejoice before the Lord your God seven days." Each day of the feast a circuit (*haqqafah*) is made during the service with the Lulab in the right hand and Ethrog in the left, while reciting the prayers; beginning and closing with the invocation "Hosanna." On the seventh day seven such processions take place and willow branches are beaten on the benches, and this day is therefore called *Hosannah Rabbah*, the day of the great *Hosanna*.

MANUSCRIPT COPY OF THE BOOK OF ESTHER, written on parchment, with hand-painted views illustrating the events narrated in the book.— The Book of Esther is usually called Megilla (roll), or more fully *Megillath Esther* (roll of Esther). It is read in the Synagogue on the feast of *Purim*, on the 15th of *Adar* (March-April), established to commemorate the deliverance of the Jews from the machinations of Haman related in this book. It is one of the "five rolls" (*hamesh megilloth*) which are read on various occasions in the Synagogue, the others being the Songs of Solomon or Canticles, Ruth, Ecclesiastes, and Lamentations.

LAMP USED AT THE FEAST OF DEDICATION (*Hanukkah*). (See plate 17, fig. 2.) The Feast of Dedication is celebrated in commemoration of the purging of the temple and restoration of the altar after Judas Maccabæus had driven out the Syrians in 164 B. C. Its institution is

---

[1] Leviticus xxiii, 14.

[2] Leviticus xxiii, 15; Deuteronomy xvi, 9.

[3] Exodus xxiii, 16.

[4] Numbers xxviii, 26; compare Exodus xxxiv, 22.

[5] Leviticus xxiii, 17. Since the dispersion Pentecost has been connected by tradition with the day on which the Law was given on Mount Sinai and the festival is called *hag mattan torah*, the feast of the giving of the law.

EXPLANATION OF PLATE 18.

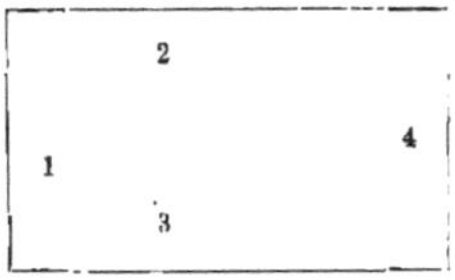

```
┌─────────────────┐
│        2        │
│                 │
│  1           4  │
│       3         │
└─────────────────┘
```

Figs. 1–3. KNIFE AND CUP OF CIRCUMCISION.
    (Cat. No. 154437, U. S. N. M. Philadelphia, Pennsylvania. Collected by Mayer Sulzberger).

Fig. 4. SPICE BOX.
    (Cat. No. 130297, U. S. N. M. Germany.)

IMPLEMENTS OF CIRCUMCISION, AND SPICE BOX.

PASSOVER PLATE.
Constantinople.
Cat. No. 130291, U.S.N.M.

OMER TABLET.
Cat. No. 151404, U.S.N.M. Deposited by David Sulzberger.

recorded in I Maccabees iv, 47–59. According to Josephus,[1] it was called "lights" (φῶτα, *phota*). In the New Testament[2] it is mentioned under the name of ἐγκαινία (*enkainia*). In the Talmud we have the legend that when the Jews entered the temple after driving out the Syrians, they found only one bottle of oil which had not been polluted, and that this was miraculously increased so as to feed the lamps of the sanctuary for eight days. The festival is held eight days, beginning with the 25th of Kislev (December-January). The principal feature of its celebration is the lighting of lights, beginning with one light on the first night and increasing the number by one light on each of the succeeding nights. The specimen is probably of Dutch make and exhibits an interesting survival of the ancient Roman lamps.

KNIFE AND CUP USED AT CIRCUMCISION. (See plate 18, fig. 1.) The rite of circumcision (*milah*) is practiced in pursuance of Genesis xvii, 10–12: "This is My covenant, which ye shall keep, between Me and you and thy seed after thee; every male among you shall be circumcised. And ye shall be circumcised in the flesh of your foreskin; and it shall be a token of a covenant betwixt me and you. And he that is eight days old shall be circumcised among you, every male throughout your generations." In early times circumcision was performed with stone knives.[3] The later Jews used iron or steel knives. With the performance of the rite of circumcision was combined the naming of the child.[4] Circumcision was common in Egypt as early as the fourth dynasty.[5] At the present day it prevails among the Kaffirs and some negro tribes of Africa, in parts of Australia, in many of the South Sea Islands, and it is said to be practiced by the Abyssinian Christians as a national custom. Early Spanish travelers found it to be prevalent in the West Indies, Mexico, and among tribes in South America. It is a common rite among Mohammedans everywhere.

GARMENT OF FRINGES (*Arba' Kanfoth*).—This garment is worn by men in pursuance of the command[6] "Thou shalt make thee fringes upon the four borders of thy vesture, wherewith thou coverest thyself." It is usually made of wool, with fringes attached to the four corners, and is worn over the shoulders, underneath the ordinary outer garment.

PHYLACTERIES (*tefillin*). (See plate 21.)—Used by Jewish males after they attain the age of 13 years and a day, at morning prayers, except on Saturday and other feast days. These objects are employed in the Jewish ritual in pursuance of the command that the words of God should be "a sign upon your hand, and for frontlets between your eyes."[7] They consist of parchment cases containing the passages

---

[1] Antiquities xii, 7, 7.
[2] John x, 22.
[3] Compare Exodus iv, 246 ("flint"); Joshua v, 2 ("knives of flint").
[4] Luke i, 59; ii, 21.
[5] Compare Herodotus ii, 36, 37, 104; Wilkinson, Ancient Egypt, ch. xv.
[6] Numbers xv, 37–41, and Deuteronomy xxii, 12.
[7] Exodus xiii, 9–10, and Deuteronomy xi, 18.

Deuteronomy vi, 4-9, and xi, 13-21, written on slips of parchment, attached to leather straps for binding on the forehead and left arm. In the case for the head the passages are written on four separate strips, and in the case for the hand on one piece of parchment, and put into a square case. They are called *tefillin* in the Talmud, a word derived from *tefillah* (prayer). The New Testament refers to their ostentatious use.[1]

SILK PRAYER SHAWL (*Tallith*).—The *tallith* is a kind of prayer shawl made of silk, wool, or linen, with çiçith or fringes fastened to the four corners, worn by men at the morning services. It is usually adorned with horizontal stripes of blue or purple; the Jews in the Orient substitute for these stripes a blue ribband worked in the corners. The wearing of a garment with fringes is commanded.[2] In ancient times this garment, it seems, was worn as an outer robe.[3] At present the Jews wear, besides the tallith, a kind of vest with fringes under the upper garments, which is called the "small tallith" (*tallith katon*), or the "four corners" (*arba' kanfoth*).

GOLD WEDDING RING. (See plate 11, fig. 2.) The Jewish marriage is made valid by the *Kiddushin*, i. e., by the bridegroom putting a ring on the hand of the bride while saying the words: "Behold, thou art wedded to me by this ring according to the law of Moses and Israel."

MARRIAGE CONTRACT (*kethubah*), written on parchment and illuminated. (See plate 22.) In the *kethubah*, or marriage contract, are recorded the obligations of the husband and the amount of the dowry allowed the bride. There is an established form of the *kethubah* usually beginning with the words: "Under good auspices, and with good luck to bridegroom and bride, 'Whoso findeth a wife findeth a good thing, and obtaineth favor of the Lord.'"[4] The husband pledges himself to love and honor his wife and to provide for her becomingly. The minimum of the dowry is fixed by the law to be 200 shekels (about $50) for a virgin and 100 (about $25) for a widow or divorced woman. To this is usually added what the bride has received from her parents and what the husband settles on her voluntarily, all of which she gets in case of the death of the husband, or of divorce. The contract is dated Rome, in the year of creation 5576 (1816). The contracting parties are Elijah Saki and Masal-Tob (Fortune), of Castlenuovo. The witnesses to the contract are Josua Gerson Ashkenazi and Michael Chayim Megula.

The margin is decorated with various symbolical figures, and contains the liturgy of the wedding ceremony and passages from the Bible and the Talmud referring to marriage and married life, artistically intertwined in garlands. Above, in the center, are probably the arms of the bridegroom; to the right a boy standing on a wheel pouring out the horn of plenty, with the motto, "All depends on merit and good luck;" to the left a female figure with tambourines, and the words, "Peace

---

[1] Matthew xxiii, 5.
[2] Numbers xv, 37-41; Deuteronomy xxii, 12.
[3] Matthew xxiii, 5.
[4] Proverbs xviii, 22.

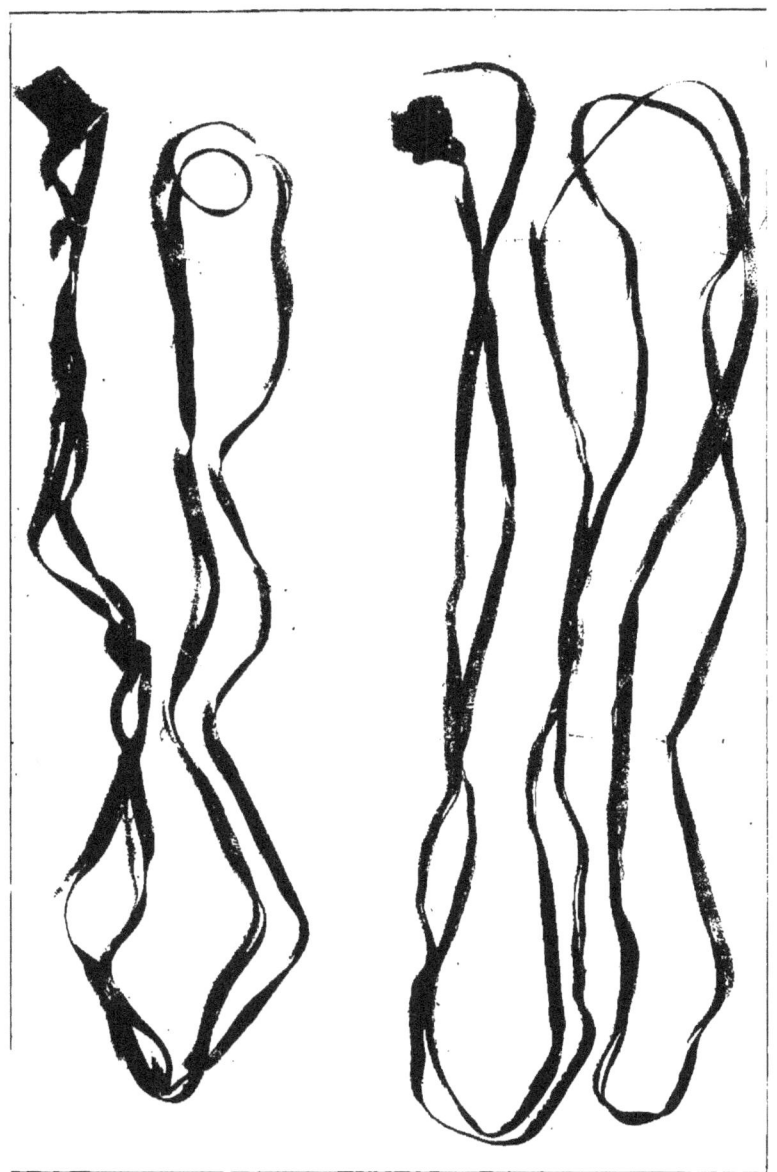

PHYLACTERIES (*Tefillin*).

Cat. No. 130276, U.S.N.M. Deposited by David Sulzberger.

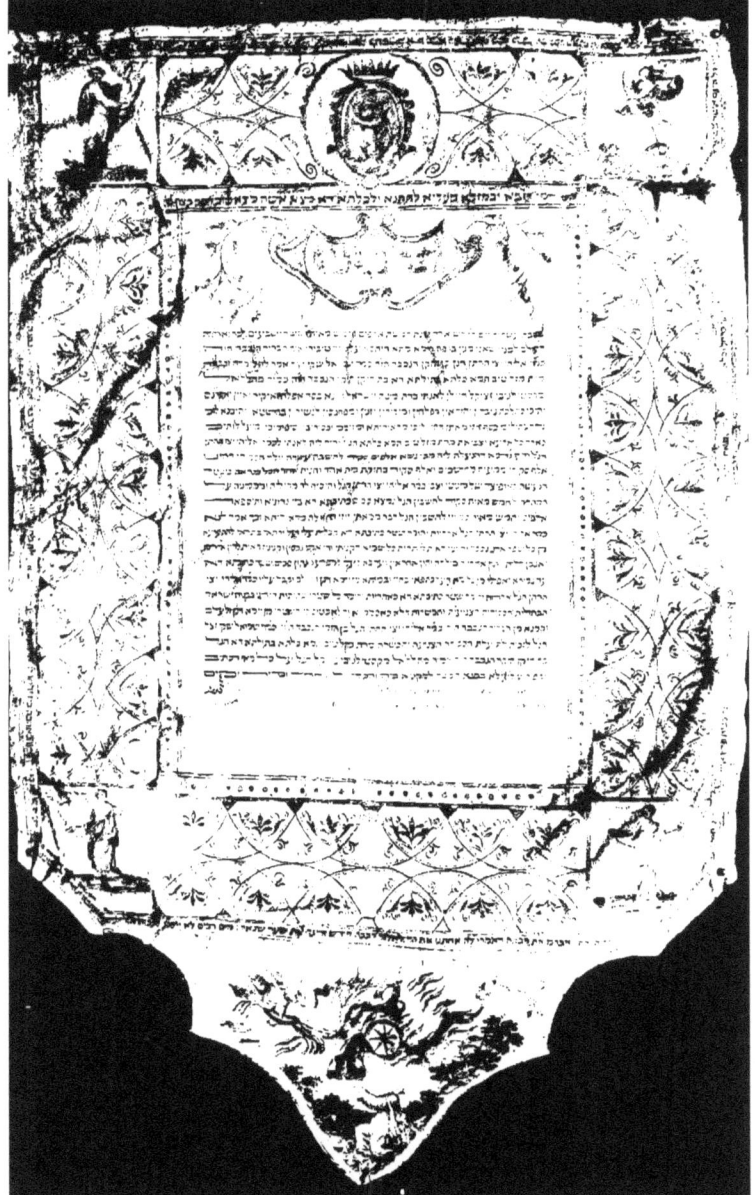

MARRIAGE CONTRACT (*Kethubah*).
Rome, Italy.
Cat. No. 154633, U.S.N.M. Collected by Dr. G. Brown Goode.

and welcome to those nigh and far." Below, to the right, is a female figure holding two burning hearts linked together by a chain, with the adage, "A well-mated couple is chosen by God" (marriages are made in heaven); to the left another female figure holding a tambourine and a flower, with a quotation from Isaiah xxxii, 8. The representation at the bottom, of Elijah ascending to heaven in a fiery chariot, his mantle falling on his disciple and successor Elisha,[1] was probably suggested by the name of the bridegroom.

MIZRACH (*the east*).—Mizrach means east, literally the place of the rising sun. There is hung in Jewish houses a tablet on the eastern wall to indicate the direction of the face when at prayer. It contains the Ten Commandments and various quotations from Scripture in Hebrew. The idea which dictates this direction is that the face shall be turned toward Jerusalem. West of Jerusalem the opposite direction would be chosen. In the temple itself the direction of prayer was toward the west, the entrance being from the east. Ancient nations that worshiped the sun turned when in prayer toward the east, the place of the rising sun. This fact is alluded to in Ezekiel viii, 16: "At the door of the temple of the Lord, between the porch and the altar, were about five and twenty men with their backs toward the temple of the Lord and their faces toward the east; and they worshiped the sun toward the east."

KNIFE WITH ITS SHEATH, used for the slaughtering of animals. (See plate 17, fig. 3.) The killing of animals for food is performed by a person especially trained and authorized, called *shochet*. The throat is cut with a long knife (*halaf*) and the internal organs are examined for traces of disease. The act of killing is called *shechita;* that of searching, *bedika*. During both acts short prayers are recited. If there be a notch (*pegima*) in the knife, or if any trace of disease be found, the animal is unfit (*terefa*) to be eaten.

ANTIQUITIES.

Next to the Israelites, with whom the Scriptures originated, the antiquities of those nations with whom Israel came in close contact, and who to a great extent influenced the course and development of the history narrated in the Bible, claim the interest of the Bible student. The exhibits in this department consisted of objects representing Egypt, Assyria, Babylonia, and the Hittites.

EGYPT.

CAST OF A BUST OF RAMSES II.—Ramses II[2] was the third king of the nineteenth dynasty and the most brilliant monarch of Egypt. He was formerly identified as the Pharaoh of the Exodus; later authorities hold that that event took place five years after his death. He was, however, in all probability, the Pharaoh of the oppression. The

---

[1] II Kings ii, 11-13.   [2] The Sesostris of the Greeks.

reasons for this supposition are that the land of Goshen in which the Israelites settled when they migrated to Egypt[1] is also called the land of Ramses, and that one of the cities which the Israelites built while in bondage was named Ramses.[2] As Ramses I reigned only for a short time, it is assumed that these names are connected with Ramses II, whose reign extended over sixty-six years in the thirteenth century B. C. (1348-1281 B. C.); and who was not only the most warlike but also the greatest builder among the Egyptian kings. The cities Pithom and Ramses which the Hebrews built for Pharaoh are thought to have been situated in the modern Wadi Tumilat. Pithom was identified in 1883 with Tell el-Maskutah in the east of this Wadi at the railroad station Ramses. Besides the building of these two cities and numerous temples, Ramses II seems also to have undertaken the continuation of the canal of the Wadi Tumilat to the Bitter Lakes, and the cutting through of the rising ground between them and the Red Sea, which connection between the Nile and the Red Sea was the true precursor of the Suez Canal.[3] The bust, which is taken from a sitting statue, represents him beardless with a helmet on his head. The original, of black granite, is in the Museum of Egyptian Antiquities in Turin, Italy.

CAST OF A RELIEF OF RAMSES II.—Photographs of the mummy of Ramses II. The mummy was discovered in July, 1881. The photographs were taken immediately after the unwinding of the mummy in June, 1886.[4]

---

[1] Genesis xlvii, 6.
[2] Exodus i, 11.
[3] Compare Adolf Erman, Life in Ancient Egypt, p. 27.
[4] Century Magazine, May, 1887. This mummy is in many ways the finest ever discovered and is of surpassing interest. Professor Maspero describes it as follows: "The head is long, and small in proportion to the body. The top of the skull is quite bare. On the temples there are a few sparse hairs, but at the poll the hair is quite thick, forming smooth straight locks about 5 centimeters in length. White at the time of death, they have been dyed a light yellow by the spices used in embalmment. The forehead is low and narrow; the brow ridge prominent; the eyebrows are thick and white; the eyes are small and close together; the nose is long, thin, arched like the noses of the Bourbons, and slightly crushed at the tip by the pressure of bandages. The temples are sunken; the cheek bones very prominent; the ears round, standing far out from the head, and pierced like those of a woman for the wearing of earrings. The jawbone is massive and strong; the chin very prominent; the mouth small, but thick-lipped and full of some kind of black paste. This paste being partly cut away with the scissors disclosed some much worn and brittle teeth, which, moreover, are white and well preserved. The mustache and beard are thin. They seemed to have been kept shaven during life, but were probably allowed to grow during the king's illness, or they may have grown after death. The hairs are white like those of the head and eyebrows, but are harsh and bristly and from 2 to 3 millimeters in length. The skin is of earthy brown, spotted with black. Finally, it may be said the face of the mummy gives a fair idea of the face of the living king. The expression is intellectual, perhaps slightly animal, but even under the somewhat grotesque disguise of mummification, there is plainly to be seen an air of sovereign majesty, of resolve and of pride."

EXHIBIT OF BIBLICAL ANTIQUITIES. 1001

The typical physiognomy of the native Egyptian, as exhibited on the numerous monuments, shows a head often too large in proportion to the body, a square and somewhat low forehead, a short and round nose, eyes large and wide open, the cheeks filled out, the lips thick, but not reversed, and the mouth somewhat wide. Contrasting the features of Ramses II with these, some scholars have assumed that he was of Semitic descent or at least had Semitic blood in his veins.

CAST OF THE HEAD OF SETI I.—The original is at the Museum of Egyptian Antiquities at Cairo, Egypt. Seti I was the second king of the nineteenth dynasty and father of Ramses II, the Pharaoh of the oppression. He reigned for about twenty-seven years in the thirteenth century B. C.

CAST OF A RELIEF OF SETI I.—Photograph of the mummy of Seti I. Taken under the direction of Prof. G. Maspero at the Museum of Egyptian Antiquities, Cairo, Egypt.

CAST OF THE HEAD OF TIRHAKAH.—Original of granite in the Museum of Antiquities at Cairo. King of Egypt and Ethiopia, 698-672 B. C. According to the Biblical account,[1] Tirhakah, "King of Ethiopia" (in Egyptian Taharqa), encountered Senacherib, King of Assyria, while the latter was on his expedition against Judah. From the Cuneiform inscriptions we learn that Tirhakah entered into an alliance with Baal, King of Tyre, against Assyria. Hezekiah, King of Judah, also joined the league. Esarhaddon marched into Egypt, and putting Tirhakah to flight he placed the rule of the whole country under twenty vassals loyal to Assyria. On the death of Esarhaddon, Tirhakah returned to Egypt, drove out the Assyrians that were there, and took possession of Memphis. Assurbanipal, the son and successor of Esarhaddon (668-626 B. C.), at once went to Egypt and defeated him at Karbanit. Tirhakah was again obliged to flee to Thebes and thence to Nubia. The twenty vassal kings were restored and Necho (*Niku*), "King of Sais and Memphis" put at their head. Soon after this Necho headed a rebellion against the Assyrian rule, but the plot was suppressed by the Assyrian garrison of Egypt and Necho sent in chains to Nineveh. But when Assurbanipal heard of the new successes of Tirhakah in Egypt, he sent Necho back to rule over all Egypt under the direction of Assyria. Tirhakah soon afterwards died. Manetho, who calls him *Tarkos* (*Tarakos*), says he was the last king of the twenty-fifth dynasty. Strabo (xvi, I, 6) calls him *Tearkon*, and describes him as one of the greatest conquerors of the ancient world.

MUMMY.—Length, 5 feet 6 inches. Found at Luxor, Egypt, in 1886. (See plates 23 and 24.) No hieroglyphics or inscriptions exist either on the mummy or outer case. The face and head are covered with a mask of green cement, the body delicately proportioned. On the chest lie four small tablets about the size of playing cards, each one having a mummied figure of Osiris in a standing position. Two shield-shaped

---

[1] II Kings xix, 9, and Isaiah xxxvii, 9.

ornaments lie across the breast and stomach, respectively. The upper one bears the sacred beetle with spread wings, beneath which is a nilometer standing between two figures, which support each a globe upon the head. The faces of these figures are covered with square pieces of gold leaf. At the end of the wings is represented the hawk-head of Ra, also supporting a globe. Over the surface of the shield are painted representations of jewelry. On the lower shield appears a kneeling figure of Nephthys, with extended arms and wings. Upon her head she wears a headband supporting a globe. On either side of the head are two groups, each containing three small figures. Ostrich plumes appear in the corner of the shield. Along the legs is a sheet of cemented linen, on the top of which is a mummy on a dog-shaped bier; at the head of the bier is a figure kneeling, holding an ostrich plume; below this is a group of seven kneeling figures holding plumes. Further down is a second nilometer, on either side of which a figure with an implement in each hand faces two mummied figures, both of which have the faces concealed with a square patch of gold leaf. The feet are incased in a covering of cemented linen.

The Egyptians conceived man as consisting of at least three parts—the body, the soul, and the *Ka*, i. e., the double or genius. The *Ka* was supposed to remain in existence after death, and to be the representative of the human personality. In order that the *Ka* might take possession of the body when it pleased, the body had to be preserved from decay. The preservation of the body was accordingly the chief end of every Egyptian who wished for everlasting life. To this end the Egyptians mummified their bodies, built indestructible tombs, inscribed the tombs and coffins with magical formulæ to repel the attacks of the demons, and placed statutes, household goods, food, statuettes of servants, etc., that the tomb might resemble as much as possible the old home of the deceased.[1] The process of mummifying the bodies by various methods of embalming was of high antiquity in Egypt, probably going back to the earliest dynasties; the oldest mummy which was found at Saqqarah in 1881, and is now at the museum of Gizeh, dates from 3200 B. C. This practice is said to have continued to 500 A. D. The art reached the highest point at Thebes during the eighteenth and nineteenth dynasties, when spices and aromatic substances were used, and the skin of the bodies so prepared as to retain a slight color and a certain flexibility. What is known of the process is derived chiefly from the Greek writers Herodotus[2] and Diodorus Siculus,[3] and from examinations of the mummies themselves. According to these sources the Egyptians employed three methods of embalming, of more or less elaborateness, according to the wealth and position of the deceased. The most costly mode is estimated by Diodorus at a talent of silver—about $1,250. The embalmers first removed part of the brain through the nostrils by means of an iron hook,

---

[1] Compare Adolf Erman, Life in Ancient Egypt, p. 306.   [2] Book ii 85.   [3] Book i 91.

MUMMY AND COVER OF COFFIN.
Luxor, Egypt.
Cat. No. 150790, U.S.N.M.   Gift of Hon. S. S. Cox, U. S. Minister to Turkey.

MUMMY CASE

destroying the rest by the infusion of caustic drugs. An incision was then made in the side with a sharp Ethiopian stone and the intestines removed. The abdomen was rinsed with palm wine and sprinkled with powdered perfumes. It was then filled with pure myrrh pounded, cassia, and other aromatics, frankincense excepted, and sewn up again. The body was then steeped in natron (subcarbonate of soda) for seventy days, afterwards washed and swathed in strips of linen and smeared with gum. The second mode of embalming cost about 20 minae—about $300. In this case cedar oil was injected into the abdomen. The oil was prevented from escaping, and the body steeped in natron for the prescribed time. On the last day the cedar oil was let out from the abdomen, carrying with it the intestines in a state of dissolution, while the flesh was consumed by the natron, so that nothing was left but the skin and bones. The third method, which was used for the poorer classes, consisted in rinsing the abdomen with syrmaea, an infusion of senna and cassia, and steeping the body for the usual period in natron. Examinations of Egyptian mummies have proven the accounts of Herodotus and Diodorus to be in the main correct. For mummies, both with and without ventral incisions, are found, and some are preserved by means of balsams and gums, and others by bitumen and natrum, and the hundreds of skulls of mummies which are found at Thebes contain absolutely nothing, while other skulls are found to be filled with bitumen, linen rags, and resin. The term "mummy" is derived from the Arabic *mumiya*, "bitumen" and the Arabic word for mummy is *mumiyya* "bitumenized thing." The native Egyptian word for mummy is *sahu*.[1] In the Bible, instances of embalming are only met with in connection with the Egyptians, the bodies of Jacob and Joseph, who died in Egypt, being thus treated.[2]

MODEL OF A MUMMY. (See plate 25.) Small wooden figure in mummy case. They perhaps represent the servants who accompanied their master in the realm of the departed in order to wait on him there, and were termed by the Egyptians "answerers" (*ushebte*), i. e., those who would answer for the departed and perform the work for him.[3]

FRAGMENTS OF MUMMIED DOG, CAT, CROCODILE, AND OTHER ANIMALS. (See plate 25.) The Egyptians believed that their several divinities assumed the forms of various animals; so, for instance, Ptah appears as the Apis-bull, Amon as a ram, Sebek is represented as a crocodile-headed man, Bastis as a cat-headed woman, etc. These animals are therefore venerated as the manifestations or symbols of the respective divinities, and the willful killing of one of them was a capital offense. These sacred animals were embalmed and buried in graves. Thus, at Bubastis, the center of the worship of the goddess Bast, was

---

[1] E. A. Wallis Budge, The Mummy, 1893, p. 173.
[2] Genesis L, 2-26.
[3] Adolf Erman, Life in Ancient Egypt, p. 317, and E. A. W. Budge, The Mummy, pp. 211-215.

a special cemetery for cats, which was recently identified at the modern Zagazig. Diodorus Siculus says[1] that when a cat died all the inmates of the house shaved their eyebrows as a sign of mourning.[2]

BOOK OF THE DEAD.—A series of original fragments and a facsimile of an Egyptian papyrus at the British Museum in London. The so-called Egyptian "Books of the Dead" are collections of religious texts, hymns, invocations, prayers to the gods, etc., intended for the use and protection of the dead in the world beyond the grave. The original of the one referred to was found in the tomb of Ani, "Royal Scribe" and Scribe of the Sacred Revenue of all the gods of Thebes, "who is accompanied on his way through the divers parts of the realm of the dead by his wife, Tutu. The hieroglyphic text is accompanied by colored vignettes, which depict the various scenes through which the deceased has to pass in the nether world, as his appearance before Osiris, the Supreme Judge of the dead, the weighing of the heart of the departed against the goddess of Truth, etc. The prayers and magical formulæ were written out on a roll of papyrus and bound up inside the bandages of the mummy.

TWO SCARABAEI.—The *Scarabæus Aegyptiorum*, or *Ateuchus Sacer*, that is, the great cockchafer found in tropical countries, was regarded in Egypt as the symbol of the god Kheper, who was termed by the Egyptians "the father of the gods," and who was later identified with the rising sun. As the sun by his daily revolution and reappearance typified the return of the soul to the body, the scarabæus, which is in Egyptian likewise called Kheper, was the emblem of the revivication of the body and the immortality of the soul. Models of Scarabæi, made of various kinds of materials, usually inscribed with names of gods, kings, and other persons, and with magical legends and devices, were buried with the mummies (placed on the heart or the finger of the dead) and were also worn by the living, principally as charms. The insects themselves have also been found in coffins.

EGYPTIAN BRICK.—Sun-baked brick from an early tomb, Thebes, Egypt. The usual dimensions of an Egyptian brick was from 20 or 17 to $14\frac{1}{2}$ inches in length, $8\frac{3}{4}$ to $6\frac{1}{2}$ inches in width, and 7 to $4\frac{1}{2}$ inches thick. It consists of ordinary soil mixed with chopped straw and sun-baked. This method of making bricks is alluded to in Exodus v, 18, where the oppressed Israelites are told " there shall no straw be given you, yet shall ye deliver the tale of bricks." In the ruins of Pithom, one of the cities in which the Israelites were employed, three kinds of brick were discovered, some with stubble, some with straw, and some without. Among the paintings of Thebes, one on a tomb represents brickmaking captives with "taskmasters," who, armed with sticks, are receiving the "tale of bricks" and urging on the work. Judging from the monuments, the process of making sun-dried bricks was much the same as in modern times. The clay or mud was mixed with the neces-

---

[1] Book i, 83.   [2] E. A. W. Budge, The Mummy, pp. 355–358.

MODEL OF A MUMMY AND FRAGMENTS OF MUMMIED ANIMALS.
Egypt.
Cat. No. 1565, U.S.N.M. Collected by George R. Gliddon.

sary amount of straw or stubble by treading it down in a shallow pit. The prepared clay was carried in hods upon the shoulders and shaped into bricks of various sizes.[1]

MODERN EGYPTIAN BRICK FROM THEBES.—Of the same general make and character as the ancient specimen.

EGYPTIAN COTTON.—Cotton of a very fine grade is now grown in Egypt. The question as to whether it was known or extensively used in that country, or in other lands bordering on the Mediterranean, is one that has given rise to much discussion. Authorities on the cotton plant have definitely asserted that it was well known in Egypt from early times; thus M. Jardin[2] states that it is certain that the cotton plant existed in Upper Egypt, Nubia, and Abyssinia in the wild state; that it was known to the ancient Egyptians, and that the proof of its existence is the finding of some seeds of *Gossypium Arboreum*, by Rosellini, in the coffin of a mummy. He further holds the opinion that linen and cotton were simultaneously employed in Egypt, but that the former was more costly than the latter and was reserved for purposes relating to the cult. In the valuable work on the Cotton Plant issued by the United States Department of Agriculture,[3] Mr. R. B. Handy, the author of a chapter on the Ancient History of Cotton, holds practically the same view.[4] On the other hand, it has been claimed by some authors that cotton was quite unknown in Egypt, a fact largely based upon the conclusions arrived at by James Thomson in an article on the "Mummy Cloths of Egypt."[5] Mr. Thomson, after twelve years' study of the subject, reached the opinion that the bandages of the mummy were universally made of linen. It would appear that cotton was not well known to the ancient Israelites, for we find it mentioned but once in the Bible, in the Book of Esther,[6] which, of course, has a Persian background and contains a description of a Persian palace. The passage reads: "In the court of the garden of the King's Palace there were hangings of white and violet-colored cotton cloths fastened with cords of fine linen and purple to silver rings and pillars of marble." The Hebrew word translated "cotton" is "karpas," derived from the Sanskrit "karpasa."

Between the extremes of opinion, the truth seems to be that cotton was indigenous in India and that its products made their way gradually, through commerce, to the Mediterranean countries and that the plant itself followed gradually either through commerce or by way of Persia. It is plain that the cotton plant existed in Egypt in the time of Pliny

---

[1] Adolf Erman, Life in Ancient Egypt, p. 417.
[2] Le Cotton, pp. 10, 11.
[3] Bulletin 33, Office of Experiment Station.
[4] See also the Descriptive Catalogue of Useful Fiber Plants of the World, by Charles Richards Dodge, issued by the Department of Agriculture, 1897.
[5] London and Edinburg Philosophical Magazine, 3d ser., V, p. 355, cited by Budge in The Mummy, p. 190.
[6] Chapter I, verses 5, 6.

(the first century of the Christian era), and it also seems likely that inasmuch as there is no representation whatsoever on any Egyptian monuments thus far found, or on any monuments found in Western Asia, of a cotton plant, that it was not known in that country in early days. It is difficult to conclude that so striking an object would not have been depicted on the monuments, when the ancient artists found it possible to figure so many of the various plants known to them.

ASSYRIA AND BABYLONIA.

Illustrating these countries the following specimens were shown:

CAST OF THE SO-CALLED OVAL OF SARGON.—The original is a small egg-shaped piece of veined marble, pierced lengthwise. It was discovered by Mr. Hormuzd Rassam at Abu-Habba, Babylonian *Sippar* (in the Bible *Sepharvaim*), a city from which the King of Assyria transported colonists to Samaria. The inscription reads: "I, Sargon, the king of the city, King of Agade, have dedicated this to the Sun-god (Samas) of Sippar." This king is supposed to have reigned about 3,800 B. C., and the object is no doubt a contemporary document. The date is derived from a statement on the cylinder of Nabonidus found at the same place. Nabonidus, the last King of Babylon (555–538 B. C.), the father of Belshazzar, records that when rebuilding the Temple of the Sun-god he found the original foundation stone of Naram-Sin, Sargon's son, which none of his predecessors had seen for 3200 years. Agade, mentioned on the Oval of Sargon, is Akkad, enumerated in the genealogical tablet[1] as one of the four cities of Nimrod's empire. Akkad was also the name of the entire district of North Babylonia.[2]

MODEL OF A TEMPLE TOWER OF BABYLON.—The model is plaster, painted, and was made after the descriptions of the Temple Tower of Borsippa, on the scale of one-fourth inch to the foot. (See plate 26.) From the most ancient times the principal cities of Mesopotamia had towers. These were used as observatories, also for the performance of religious ceremonies, and perhaps in early times for military defense. In Genesis xi, 1–9, it is related that certain immigrants began to build in the plain of Shinear a city and a tower, which was left incomplete in consequence of the confusion of tongues, and the city was thence called Babel (confusion). This "Tower of Babel" has been connected both by Arab tradition and on the authority of archaeologists with the imposing ruins of Birs-Nimrud ("Nimrod's Tower") on the site of the Temple Tower of Nebo, at Borsippa, which was a surburb of the city of Babylon, and which in the cuneiform inscriptions is called "Babylon the Second." This Temple Tower of Borsippa, termed in the inscriptions *E-zida* ("the eternal house"), was a perfect type of these edifices, and it has been suggested as probable that the Tower of Babel men-

---
[1] Genesis x, 10.
[2] Proc. Society of Biblical Archaeology, VI, p. 68; VII, p. 66; VIII, p. 243.

MODEL OF A BABYLONIAN TEMPLE TOWER.
Made in the U. S. National Museum.
Cat. No. 150:3, U.S.N.M.

tioned in Genesis was conceived on the same plan. The Temple of Borsippa was reconstructed with great splendor by Nebuchadnezzar (604–561 B. C.), but he made no changes in the general character and plan. According to the description of Herodotus,[1] who mistakes it for the Temple of Bel, and the report of Sir Henry Rawlinson, who carefully examined the mound of Birs-Nimrud, the Tower of Borsippa appears to have been constructed on the plan of a step-shaped or terraced pyramid. Such stepped pyramids have not only survived in Egypt, in the Great Pyramid of Sakkarah, but are also found in Mexico (at Cholula, City of Mexico, etc.), where they are called *Teocallis*—i. e., "houses of god"—consisting of terraced structures, five to seven stories high, and surmounted by a chamber or cell, which is the temple itself. It is assumed that these temple towers were the prototype of the later Egyptian pyramids, the stories disappearing in the latter by filling up the platforms of the different stages, which produced an uninterrupted slope on all sides. The Temple Tower of Nebo, at Borsippa, was built in seven stages, whence it is sometimes called in the inscriptions "Temple of the seven spheres of heaven and earth." Upon an artificial terrace of burnt bricks rose the first stage, 272 feet square; on this the second, 230 feet square; then the third, 188 feet square, each of these three lower stages being 26 feet high. The height of each of the four upper stories was 15 feet, while their width was 146, 104, 62, and 20 feet, respectively, so that the whole edifice, not including the artificial terrace, had a height of about 140 feet. The several stages were faced with enameled bricks in the colors attributed to the different planets, the first story, representing Saturn, in black; then, in order, Jupiter, orange; Mars, red; the Sun, thought to have been originally plated with gold; Venus, white; Mercury, blue, and the seventh, dedicated to the Moon, the head of the Babylonian pantheon, was plated with silver. The floors of the platforms were probably inlaid with mosaics. The whole structure terminated in a chapel placed on the central axis of the tower and surmounted by a cupola. According to Herodotus there stood in the spacious sanctuary on the top of the tower a couch of unusual size, richly adorned, with a golden table by its side. But no statue of any kind was set up in the chamber, nor was it occupied at night by anyone but a native woman. The top stage was also used as an observatory. Double converging stairs or gently ascending ramps led up to the several platforms.

THE CHALDEAN DELUGE TABLET.—Containing the cuneiform text of the Babylonian account of the Deluge as restored by Prof. Paul Haupt. Engraved in clay under the direction of Professor Haupt, by Dr. R. Zehnpfund, of Rosslau, Germany. Measurement, $8\frac{3}{8}$ by $6\frac{3}{8}$ inches. The Babylonian story of the Deluge is contained in the eleventh tablet of the so-called Izdubar or Gilgamesh[2] legends, commonly known under the name of the Babylonian Nimrod Epic. The Babylonian

---

[1] Book i, 181–183. [2] This name is also read by some Gizdubar and Gibel-gamesh.

narrative of the Deluge closely accords both in matter and language with the biblical account as contained in Genesis vi–viii. Xisuthrus or Hasisadra, the hero of the Babylonian account, corresponding to the Biblical Noah, is informed by a god of the coming flood and ordered to build a ship to preserve himself, his family, and friends, and various animals. After he had sent out divers birds (a dove, swallow, and raven) he landed on the mountain Nizir, in Armenia, and offers a sacrifice to the gods, after which he is transferred to live with the gods. The originals were found during the British excavations in the Valley of the Euphrates and Tigris, and are now preserved in the British Museum, in London. There was also exhibited a cast of some of the original fragments now preserved in the British Museum.

CAST OF A COLOSSAL HUMAN-HEADED WINGED LION, 11 by 9 feet; original of yellow limestone in the British Museum. It was found by Sir Austen H. Layard in 1846 at Kuyunjik on the site of ancient Nineveh, and is supposed to belong to the period of Asurnazirpal, who reigned 884–860 B. C. Figures of composite animals of stone or metal, sometimes of colossal size, were placed by the Assyrians at the entrances to the temples of the gods and the palaces of the kings. They were considered as emblems of divine power, or genii (Assyrian, *shedu*), and believed to "exclude all evil." Lions were also placed "beside the stays" and on either side of the steps of the gilded ivory throne of Solomon.[1] Some Assyriologists connect the Assyrian winged and composite beings with those seen by the prophet Ezekiel in his vision of the "chariot," as described in the first chapter of his prophecies, and the cherubim guarding the entrance to the Garden of Eden[2] and those carved on the Ark of the Covenant.[3] Parallels are also found in the religious figures of other peoples, as the sphinx of the Egyptians and Persians, the chimera of the Greeks, and the griffin of northeastern mythology. It would seem that the composite creature form was intended to symbolize either the attributes of divine essence or the vast powers of nature as transcending that of individual creatures.

The winged lion, called "Nergal," was also sacred to Anatis and to Beltis, the goddess of war.

CAST OF THE BLACK OBELISK OF SHALMANESER II, King of Assyria 860–824 B. C. The original of black basalt, which is now preserved in the British Museum, was accidentally discovered by Sir Austen Henry Layard at Nimrud, on the site of the Biblical Calah,[4] about 19 miles below Nineveh. The obelisk is about 7 feet high. The terraced top and the base are covered with cuneiform script containing a record of Shalmaneser's campaigns nearly to the last year of his long

---

[1] I Kings x, 19, 20.
[2] Genesis iii, 24.
[3] Exodus xxv, 18, etc. Compare also the "four living creatures" in Revelations v, 14; vi, 1.
[4] Genesis x, 12.

reign. The upper part is occupied by five compartments of bas-reliefs running in horizontal bands around the four sides, and representing processions of tribute bearers from five nations. Narrow bands between the compartments contain short legends descriptive of the scenes represented. The Black Obelisk and the other monuments of Shalmaneser II supplement the Biblical narrative We learn from them that he was the first Assyrian king, so far as is yet known, to come into relations with Israel. Among the tribute bearers represented on the obelisk are Israelites, and in the second row is a legend reading, "Tribute of Ya'ua, son of Humri: silver, gold, vials of gold, cups of gold, pans of gold, vessels of gold, of lead, scepters for the King's hand, axes I received."[1] In the record of the sixth year of his reign (854 B. C.) Shalmaneser relates his victorious campaign against Benhadad, King of Damascus (in the inscription Dadidri), Ishiluna of Hamat, and their confederate kings. From another inscription engraved by Shalmaneser in the rocks of Armenia it is learned that one of the allies of this great coalition led by Benhadad against Assyria was Ahab, King of Israel (in the Assyrian inscription Ahabbu Sirlai), who had furnished 2,000 chariots and 10,000 soldiers. Neither of these facts—the participation of Ahab in the Syrian league and the payment of tribute to Shalmaneser by Jehu—is recorded in the Bible. This King is not to be confounded with Shalmaneser IV (727-722 B. C.), who is mentioned in II Kings xviii, 9, in connection with the conquest of Samaria.[2]

CAST OF A BELL, the original of which is in the Royal Museum of Berlin. The bell is decorated in bas-relief with the figure of Ea, the Assyro-Babylonian divinity of the ocean, also called the "Lord of Profound Wisdom," and hence considered as the god of science and culture. He is represented in human form covered over by a fish. He is probably identical with the Oannes, described by the Chaldean priest Berosus as the founder of civilization. Through a mistaken etymology of Dagon from Hebrew *dag*, fish, the Philistine divinity of that name, mentioned in I Samuel v, was thought to have been a fish god and identified with the water god Ea. Dagon was also a divinity of the Assyro-Babylonians, known by the name of Dagan, but had no connection with the water. He was considered by the Phenicians and, therefore, presumably, by the Philistines also, as the god of agriculture.[3] Besides the representation of Ea, there are also on the bell figures of several demons and a priest.

---

[1] II Kings ix and x.
[2] This monument is described by Theo. G. Pinches, British Museum, Guide to the Nimroud Central Saloon, 1886, pp. 26–45; the inscription is translated by Dr. Edward Hincks, Dublin University Magazine, XLII, 1853, pp. 420–426; A. H. Sayce, Records of the Past, V, pp. 27–42.
[3] See A. H. Sayce, Hibbert Lectures on the Religion of the Ancient Babylonians, pp. 188, 189, and in Smith's Dictionary of the Bible under *Dagon*, and The Sunday School Times, May 27, 1893.

THE HITTITES.

The Hittites (Hebrew *Hittim*) are derived in the Bible from Heth, son of Canaan, the son of Ham.[1] They are depicted as an important tribe settled in the region of Hebron on the hill,[2] and are often mentioned as one of the seven principal Canaanitish tribes, and sometimes as comprising the whole Canaanitish population.[3]

From Abraham to Solomon the Hittites came more or less in contact with Israel. Numbers of them remained with the Jews even as late as the time of Ezra and Nehemiah.[4] Hittite kings are mentioned as settled north of Palestine,[5] and some scholars distinguish the latter as Syrian Hittites from the Canaanite tribe. Recently the Hittites have been identified with the *Cheta* of the Egyptian and *Chatti* of the Assyrian monuments.

From the notices on these monuments it is gathered that this people at an early period constituted a mighty power, dominating, for a time, the territory from the Euphrates to the Ægean, and standing forth as rivals of Egypt and Assyria. As early as the seventeenth century B. C., a struggle began for supremacy between Egypt and the Hittites, which lasted for five hundred years, when Ramses II defeated the Hittites at Kadesh, on the Orontes. He did not conquer them, however, but was compelled to make an alliance. From the twelfth to the eighth century B. C., the Hittites were in conflict with Assyria, until the Assyrian King, Sargon, put an end to the Hittite dominion in 717 B. C., when the inhabitants of Carchemish, the Hittite capital in Syria (the modern Jerablus on the Euphrates), were deported to Assyria, and the city was repeopled with Assyrian colonists.

Of late there have been added to the Biblical, Egyptian, and Assyrian sources numerous monuments which were discovered throughout Asia Minor and Northern Syria, and which are by some scholars attributed to the Hittites. The beginning was made by two Americans, Mr. J. Augustus Johnson, of the United States consular service, and Rev. S. Jessup, who in 1870 found Hittite inscriptions at Hama, in Syria. Later discoveries were made, especially by Humann and Puchstein, under the auspices of the German Government (1872), and by Ramsay and Hogarth (1890). The monuments, mostly of black basalt, contain representations in bas-relief of religious objects, winged figures, deities standing on various animals, sphinxes, gryphons, the winged disk, as symbol of the deity, the two-headed eagle (which became the standard of the Seljukian Turks, and afterwards of Austria and Russia, etc.), and inscriptions in hieroglyphic characters, written in alternating lines from right to left and left to right (*boustrophedon*). The art exhibited on these monuments is of a primitive, rude character, and recalls the early art of Babylonia, Greece, and Phenicia. The inscrip-

---

[1] Genesis x, 15.
[2] *Idem.* xxiii, 2.
[3] Joshua, 4, etc.
[4] Ezra ix, 1.
[5] I Kings x, 29; II Kings vii, 6.

tions have not yet been deciphered, and the race affinity of the Hittites and the place of their language among linguistic families are still disputed questions. Thus, J. Halevy[1] considers the originators of these monuments as Semites; P. Jensen[2] would designate them as Aryans (Cilicians), while the Italian, Cesare de Cara[3] identifies them with the Pelasgians, the ancient prehistoric inhabitants of the Grecian countries.

The pictorial representations of the Hittites, on the Egyptian as well as on their own monuments, show that they were a short, stout race, with yellow skin, receding foreheads, oblique eyes, black hair, and chin, as a rule, beardless. They wore conical caps and boots with upturned tips. These characteristics would seem to suggest that they were neither of Semitic nor Aryan origin, but belonged to the Mongolian or Turanian family, and this is as yet the more prevalent opinion.[4] The following casts of Hittite sculptures were shown:

CAST OF A COLOSSAL STATUE OF THE GOD HADAD, inscribed in the old Aramean dialect. (See plate 27.) The original of dolorite, now preserved in the Royal Museum of Berlin, was discovered by von Luschan and Humann at Gertchin, near Senjirli, which is about 70 miles to the northeast of Antioch in northern Syria. The excavations in this region were carried on by these scholars between 1888 and 1891 under the auspices of the German Oriental committee constituted for that purpose. The most important finds made during these excavations, besides the statue of Hadad, were the stele of Esarhaddon, King of Asyria, 681-668 B. C., bearing an inscription in Assyrian cuneiform writing, and a statue erected by Bar-Reknb to the memory of his father Panammu, King of Samaal, the ancient Semitic name of the region of Senjirli, inscribed, like the statue of Hadad, in the old Aramean dialect. Both these Aramean inscriptions are cut in high relief, like the hieroglyphic inscriptions on the Hittite monuments. The character of the writing resembles that of the Moabite stone and the language bears a closer resemblance to Hebrew than the Aramaic of the later period.

The statue of Hadad was erected by Panammu, son of Karul, King of Ja'di, in northern Syria, in the eighth century B. C., to the gods El, Reshef, Rakubel, Shemesh, and above all to Hadad. Hadad was the name of the supreme Syrian deity, the Baal, or Sun god, whose worship extended from Carchemish, the ancient Hittite capital in Syria, to Edom and Palestine.

Many Edomite and Syrian kings bore the name of the deity as a title.[5] In Zachariah xii, 11, there is mentioned a place in the valley of

---

[1] Revue Sémitique for 1893 and 1894.
[2] Zeitschrift der Deutschen Morgenländischen Gesellschaft XLVIII, p. 235.
[3] Gli Hethei-Pelasgi.
[4] Compare A. H. Sayce, The Hittites: the story of a forgotten Empire, London, 1888; Campbell, The Hittites, their inscriptions and their history, London, 1891; W. Wright, Empire of the Hittites, 1884.
[5] Compare Genesis xxxvi, 35; II Samuel viii, 3; Hadadezer, etc.

Megiddo named after the two Syrian divinities "Hadad-Rimmon." Coins bear the name of Abd-Hadad, "servant of Hadad," who reigned in the fourth century B. C., at Hieropolis, the later successor of Carchemish, and in the Assyrian inscriptions there occurs the abbreviated form of "Dada, god of Aleppo." Of the four other divinities named, El became the generic term for deity among Hebrews and Assyrians. Shemesh is the Sun god (Assyrian Shamash). Reshef appears to be a Hittite divinity, while Rekubel is met with here for the first time. The inscription contains thirty-four lines. The first part (lines 1 to 15) contains the dedication of Panammu to the gods to whom the monument was erected, who conferred on him the government over Ja'di, and granted the land plenty and abundance. The second part (lines 13 to 24) relates the injunction of Karul to his son Panammu, that he erect a statue to Hadad and honor him with sacrifices. The third part (lines 24 to 34) contains the usual curses against those who should destroy, deface, or carry off the monument.[1]

HITTITE DIVINITY, with trident and hammer. (See plate 28.) Cast from original of dolerite at the Royal Museum, Berlin, Germany. Found at Senjirli, Asia Minor.

HITTITE WINGED DIVINITY, with head of griffon. (See plate 29.) Cast from original of dolerite at the Royal Museum, Berlin, Germany. Found at Senjirli, Asia Minor.

HITTITE GOD OF THE CHASE, holding hares. (See plate 30.) Cast from original of dolerite at the Royal Museum, Berlin, Germany. Found at Senjirli, Asia Minor.

HITTITE FIGURE, surmounted by winged sun disk. Cast from original of calcareous rock at Boghazkeui, Asia Minor. (See plate 31.) The winged solar disk was the emblem of the supreme divinity among the Hittites, Egyptians, and Assyrians.

HITTITE WINGED SPHINX, with human head. (See plate 32.) Cast from original, of dolerite, at the Royal Museum, Berlin, Germany. Found at Senjirli, Asia Minor. It is assumed that the Hittite, not the Egyptian, form of the sphinx was the prototype of the sphinx as represented by the Greeks.

HITTITE WINGED SPHINX, with double head of man and lion. (See plate 33.) Cast from original, of dolerite, at the Royal Museum, Berlin, Germany. Found at Senjirli, Asia Minor.

HITTITE KING, in long robe, with scepter and spear. (See plate 34.) Cast from original, of dolerite, at the Royal Museum, Berlin, Germany. Found at Senjirli, Asia Minor.

THREE HITTITE WARRIORS. (See plate 35.) Cast from original, of calcarous rock, at Boghazkeui, Asia Minor. The high-peaked cap and the pointed boots seen on the figures are still in use among the peasantry in Asia Minor.

---

[1] Compare Ausgrabungen in Sendschirli I, 1893 (published by the Berlin Museum), Prof. D. H. Mueller in Zeitschrift fuer die Kunde des Morgenlandes VII, Nos. 2 and 3, and in Contemporary Review of April, 1894.

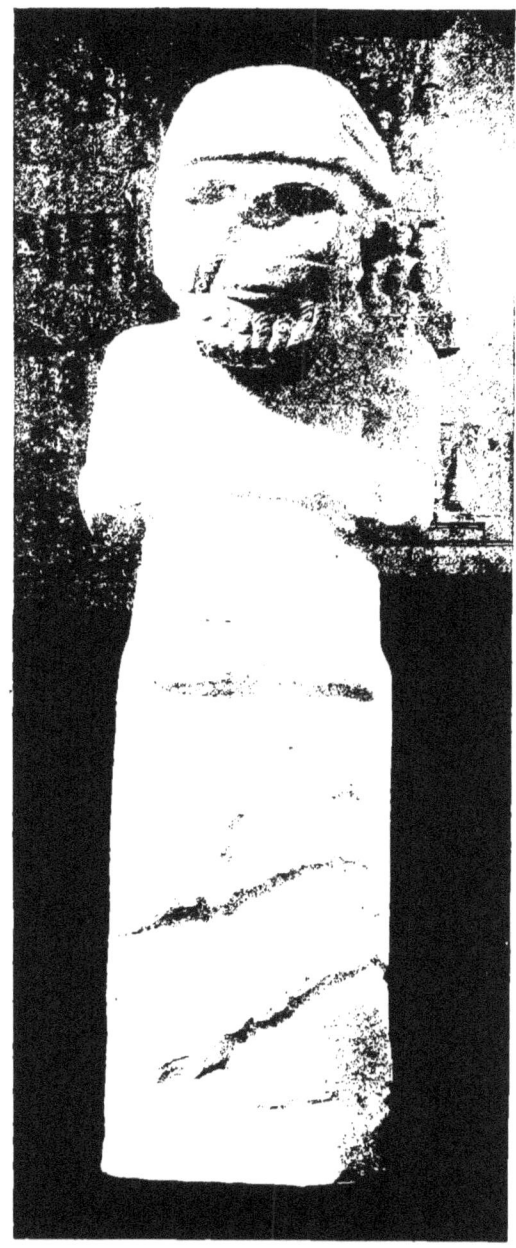

HADAD.
Gertchin, Northern Syria.
Original in Royal Museum, Berlin.
Cat. No. 155007, U.S.N.M.

HITTITE DIVINITY WITH TRIDENT AND HAMMER.
Original in Royal Museum, Berlin.
Cat. No. 155032, U.S.N.M.

HITTITE WINGED DIVINITY WITH HEAD OF GRIFFON.
Senjirli, Asia Minor.
Original in Royal Museum, Berlin.
Cat. No. 155633, U.S.N.M.

HITTITE GOD OF THE CHASE HOLDING HARES.
Senjirli, Asia Minor.
Original in Royal Museum, Berlin.
Cat. No. 155030, U.S.N.M.

HITTITE FIGURE SURMOUNTED BY WINGED SUN DISK.
Boghazkeui, Asia Minor.
Original in Royal Museum, Berlin.
Cat. No. 155015, U.S.N.M.

HITTITE WINGED SPHINX WITH DOUBLE HEAD OF MAN AND LION.
Senjirli, Asia Minor.
Original in Royal Museum, Berlin.
Cat. No. 155039, U.S.N.M.

HITTITE KING WITH SCEPTER AND SPEAR.
Senjirli, Asia Minor.
Original in Royal Museum, Berlin.
Cat. No. 155040, U.S.N.M.

HITTITE WARRIORS.
Boghazkeui, Asia Minor.
Original in Royal Museum, Berlin.
Cat. No. 155013, U.S.N.M.

HITTITE LION CHASE.
Saktschegözü.
Original in Royal Museum, Berlin.
Cat. No. 155020, U.S.N.M.

HITTITE WARRIOR WITH AX AND SWORD.
Senjirli, Asia Minor.
Original in Royal Museum, Berlin.
Cat. No. 155041, U.S.N.M.

HITTITE LUTE PLAYER.—Cast from original, of dolerite, at the Royal Museum, Berlin, Germany. Found at Senjirli, Asia Minor. (See plate 8.)

HITTITE LION CHASE. (See plate 36.) This relief, which probably served to decorate the gate of a temple or palace, plainly exhibits Assyrian influence. As on Assyrian hunting scenes, the lion is chased from a chariot occupied by the charioteer and the archer. In front of the chariot and its spirited horse the lion is attacked by two men, who drive spears in the fore and hind parts of its body. The whole scene combines archaism with vivid and powerful naturalism. The original, of granite, was found at Saktschegözu and is now in the Royal Museum of Berlin, Germany.

HITTITE WARRIOR, with ax and sword. (See plate 37.) Cast from original, of dolerite, at the Royal Museum, Berlin, Germany. Found at Senjirli, Asia Minor. The relief probably served to decorate the gate of a temple or palace.

COLLECTION OF BIBLES.

The last section of the exhibit consisted of a small collection of bibles, arranged so as to show the originals and the versions. It included manuscripts and old and rare editions of the original texts, as well as copies of the most important ancient and modern translations of the scriptures. This part of the exhibit was not only of interest to biblical students, but also served to illustrate the study of palæography.

THE OLD TESTAMENT.—The Old Testament is mainly written in the Hebrew language, which was the Semitic dialect spoken in Canaan. It is cognate to Assyrian, Arabic, Ethiopic, and Aramean, and most closely allied to Phenician and Moabite. Daniel ii, 4, to vii, 28, and Ezra iv, 8, to vi, 18, and vii, 12-26, are written in Aramean; also a few words in Genesis and Jeremiah.

The canon of the Old Testament is divided by the Jews into three portions—the law, the prophets, and the writings—and subdivided into twenty-four books. Josephus counts twenty-two books, which was followed by Origen. The fixing of the canon goes back by tradition to Ezra and the men of the great synagogue; some, however, are of the opinion that the canonicity of the prophets and writings (Greek hagiographa, or sacred writings) was settled much later. According to the present actual count the Old Testament contains thirty-nine books. This, however, does not argue a different content from ancient times—simply a further subdivision of books.

Before the Exile the books were written in the ancient Phenician characters which appear in some ancient Phenician inscriptions, on the Moabite stone, on some coins of the Maccabees, and in the Samaritan Pentateuch. In the period following the Exile and the restoration of Ezra the square letters, also called "Assyrian script," which are represented in the printed editions of the Old Testament, had gradually been introduced.

Originally the Hebrew text was written without divisions into chapters and verses, and earlier still, no doubt, without divisions into words. Great care, however, was observed to transmit the text correctly. Josephus asserts that "no one has been so bold as either to add anything to them, take anything from them, or to make any change in them" (the books of the Bible). Philo Judæus asserts that "the Jews have never altered one word of what was written by Moses," and in the Talmud a scribe is exhorted as follows: "My son, take care how thou doest thy work (for thy work is a divine one), lest thou drop or add a letter."

Nevertheless, it seems likely that errors crept into the text. Accordingly, a body of Jewish scholars known as the Massorites labored for eight centuries (the second to the tenth of the Christian era) to fix the text. They added a number of marginal readings where the text was obscure or faulty, introduced a system of punctuation and accents, and made divisions into chapters, paragraphs, and verses. They counted and recorded the number of sections, verses, words, and even letters contained in the different books. The work of the Massorites on the original text of the Old Testament closes with the schools of Aaron ben Asher in Palestine and Moses ben Napthali in Babylonia, and it is generally admitted that the text has been handed down to us in a comparatively pure and trustworthy form. The oldest complete manuscript of the Old Testament which is known dates from the year 1009 A. D.

THE NEW TESTAMENT.—The New Testament was written in Greek in its Hellenistic idiom. The original handwork of the authors perished early. The oldest manuscripts known date from the fourth century. The canon of the New Testament as it now stands and is accepted by all the churches was fixed by the councils of Hippo (393) and Carthage (397) under the influence of St. Augustine. The present division of chapters in the New Testament was originated by Cardinal Hugo of St. Caro in the thirteenth century; that of the verses was made in imitation of the Old Testament, and is first found in the Latin translation of the Vulgate, and only as late as 1551 was it placed by Robert Stephanus on the margin of the Greek text.

The following specimens were shown:

HEBREW BIBLE. Facsimile of Aleppo Codex. (See plate 38.) The original manuscript is preserved in the synagogue at Aleppo, Syria. It is assigned to Aaron ben Asher (beginning of the tenth century), and considered as one of the best authorities for the text of the Old Testament, but is probably of somewhat later origin.[1]

FRAGMENTS OF MANUSCRIPT OF THE HEBREW BIBLE. (See plates 39 and 40.) Thirteenth century. Containing a portion of the Psalms

---

[1] Wicke's Treatise on the Accentuation of the Prose Books of the Old Testament.

FACSIMILE OF ALEPPO CODEX (Genesis xxvi, 34; xxvii, 30).
Aleppo, Syria.
Cat. No. 155083, U.S.N.M.

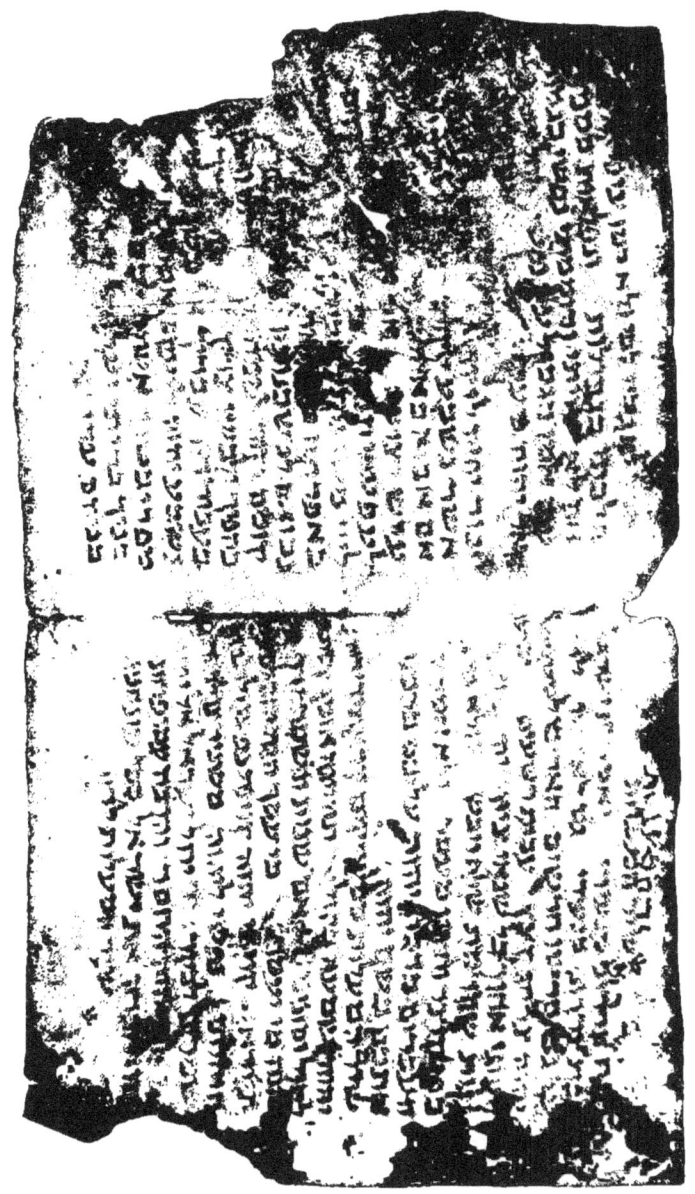

HEBREW MANUSCRIPT OF THE THIRTEENTH CENTURY (Psalms cxxix–cxxxiii).
Cairo, Egypt.
Cat. No. 165081, U.S.N.M. Deposited by Dr. Cyrus Adler.

HEBREW MANUSCRIPT OF THE THIRTEENTH CENTURY (Deuteronomy v, 1–6).
Cairo, Egypt.
Cat. No. 155081, U.S.N.M. Deposited by Dr. Cyrus Adler.

(cxxix to cxxxii, 14) and Deuteronomy v, 1-6. These were no doubt from the Genizah, since made famous by the great manuscript finds of Dr. S. Schechter, of Cambridge, England.

PRINTED EDITIONS OF THE HEBREW BIBLE.—Soon after the invention of the art of printing parts of the Old Testament were published. Thus the Psalter with Kamchis Commentary appeared in 1477 (place unknown); the Pentateuch with the Targum and the Commentary of Rashi in 1482 at Bologna, Italy. The first complete Hebrew Bible was printed at Soncino, Italy, in 1488. The second edition has neither date nor place. The third was published at Brescia, Italy, in 1494. It was the one used by Luther for his German translation. The present copy shown was a reprint, with slight alterations, of the Bible printed by Daniel Bomberg at Venice in 1517. In this edition the first effort was made to give some of the Massoretic apparatus. It contains, besides the Hebrew original, several of the Chaldean Targums and commentaries. The editor was Felix Pratensis.

HEBREW BIBLE, without vowel points, Antwerp, 1573-74.—This Bible was printed by the famous printer, Christopher Plantin (born 1514, died 1589).

HEBREW BIBLE, edited by Elias Hutter (three volumes), Hamburg, 1587.—Hutter was professor of Hebrew at Leipsic. The peculiarity of this Bible consists in the fact that the roots are printed in solid black letters, whereas the prefixes, suffixes, and formative letters (called servile letters in Hebrew grammar) are shaded.

THE HEBREW BIBLE, first American edition (see plate 41), published by Thomas Dobson, Philadelphia, 1814 (two volumes), printed by William Fry.—In 1812 Mr. Horwitz had proposed the publication of this edition of the Hebrew Bible, the first proposal of this kind in the United States. Early in 1813 he transferred his right and list of subscribers to Mr. Thomas Dobson. The work was advertised as follows in " Poulson's American Daily Advertiser," Monday, May 30, 1814:

Hebrew Bible
This day is published,
By Thomas Dobson,
No. 41, South Second Street
The First American Edition of
The Hebrew Bible,
Without the Points.

Elegantly printed by William Fry, with a new fount of Hebrew Types, cast on purpose for the work by Binney & Ronaldson, on the best superfine wove paper, two large volumes octavo.

Price in boards, Fifteen Dollars.

Subscribers will receive their copies at *Subscription Price* by applying to Thomas Dobson as above. This arduous undertaking the first of the kind attempted in the United States is now happily accomplished. The work is considered as one of the finest specimens of *Hebrew Printing* ever executed: and it is hoped will be generally encouraged by the Reverend Clergy of different denominations, and by other lovers of the Sacred Scriptures in the Hebrew Language.

POLYCHROME EDITION OF THE OLD TESTAMENT, edited by Prof. Paul Haupt, since 1892.—Some modern scholars are of the opinion that some of the books of the Old Testament as they now stand in the received text of the Massorites are composed of several sources. A company of these scholars under the editorial supervision of Prof. Paul Haupt is preparing an edition, representing by various colors the component parts as well as the portions which they consider as later additions.

LEICESTER CODEX OF THE NEW TESTAMENT. Facsimile. Original preserved in the archives of the borough of Leicester, England.—It is written in cursive script (i. e., in a continuous running hand), and is usually ascribed to the eleventh century. In the opinion of Prof. J. Rendel Harris the manuscript is of Italian origin, and no earlier than the fourteenth or even the fifteeenth century.

GREEK AND LATIN NEW TESTAMENT OF ERASMUS. (See plate 42.) Editio princeps. Printed by Frobenius in Basel, 1516.—The first complete book produced by the printing press was a Latin Bible in 1456. The Greek New Testament was first printed in the Complutensian Polyglot (so called from the Latin name of Alcala, Spain, where it was printed) of Cardinal Ximenes in 1514, but it was not issued until 1520. The edition of the Greek New Testament, by Erasmus, was, therefore, the first ever published, and became, with a few modifications, the received text printed by Elzevir in Leiden. Luther's translation was based upon it. To the Greek original Erasmus added a corrected Latin version with notes.

GREEK TESTAMENT. (See plate 43.) First American edition. Printed by Isaiah Thomas, 1800, Worcester, Massachusetts.

GREEK TESTAMENT. The second issued in America. Printed at Philadelphia by S. F. Bradford, 1806.

ANCIENT VERSIONS OF THE BIBLE.

Translations of the Scriptures became necessary when the Jews were dispersed in the Greco-Roman world and gradually abandoned the use of the Hebrew language, and later when Christianity was propagated among various nations. The oldest and most important version of the Old Testament, which in its turn became the parent of many other translations, is the Greek of Alexandria, known by the name of the Septuagint. The name Septuagint, meaning seventy, is derived from the tradition that it was made by a company of seventy (or rather seventy-two) Jewish scholars, at Alexandria, under the reign of Ptolemy Philadelphus, 285–247 B. C., who desired a copy for the library he was gathering. The truth of its origin seems to be that Alexandria became, after the Babylonian captivity, a center of Jewish

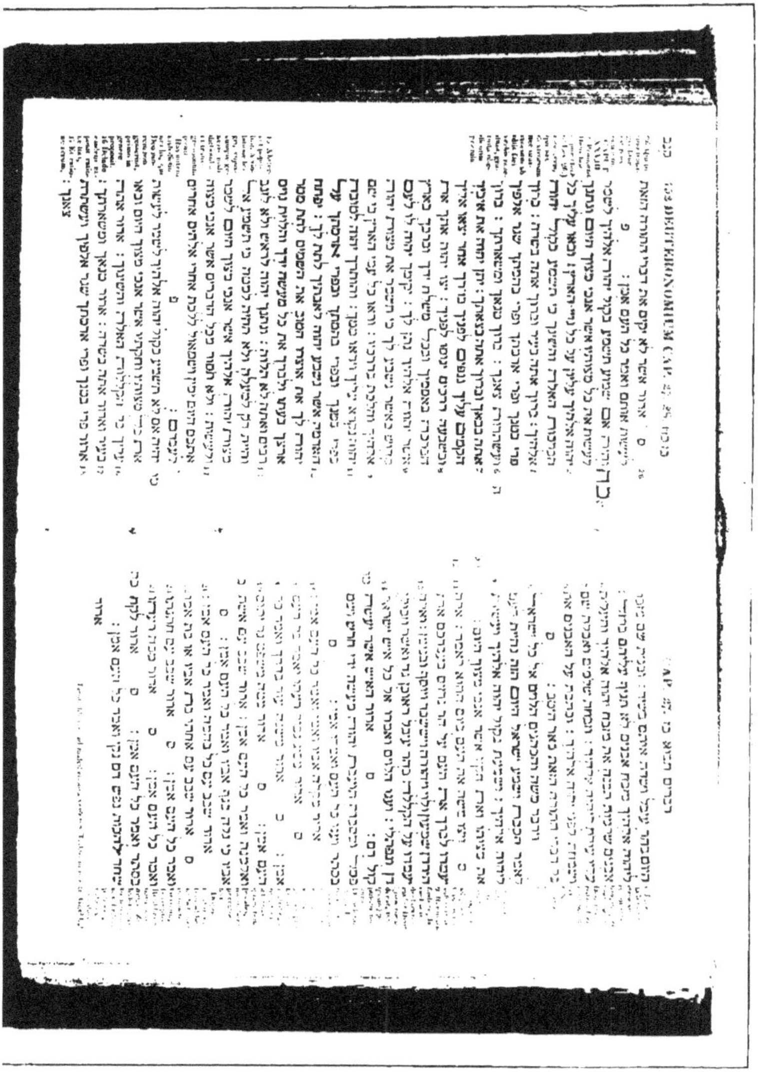

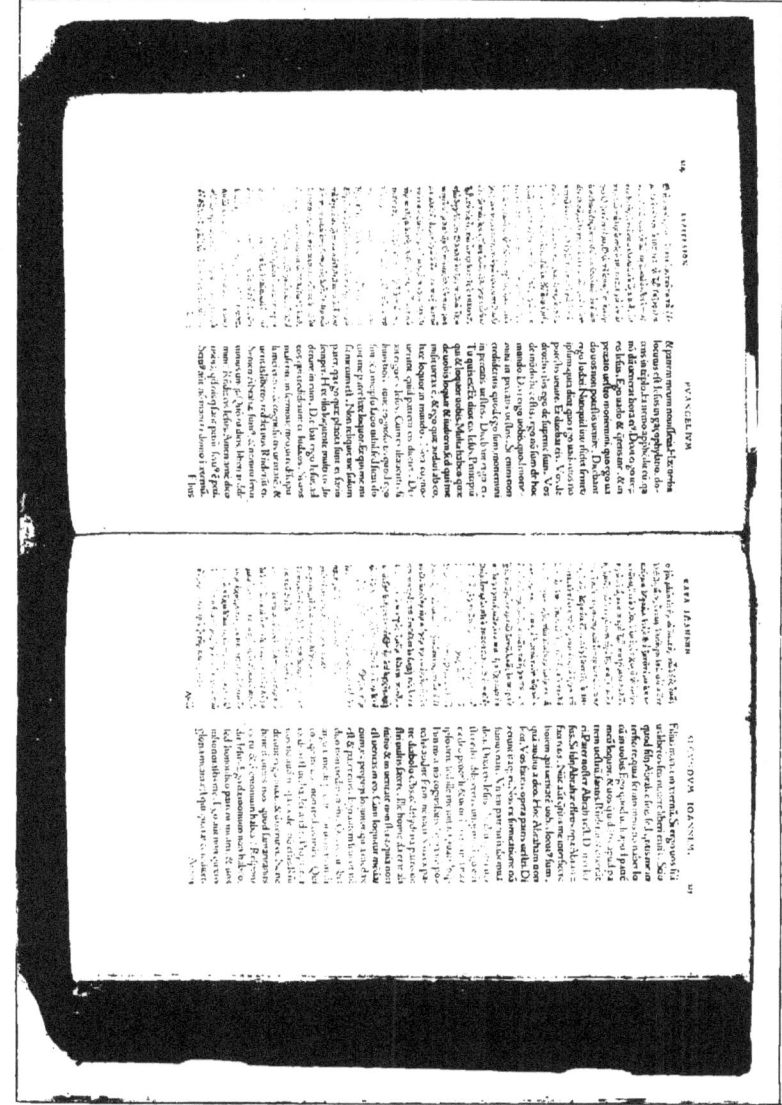

Greek and Latin New Testament of Erasmus (Gospel of John viii, 20–50).
Cat. No. 15567, U.S.N.M.

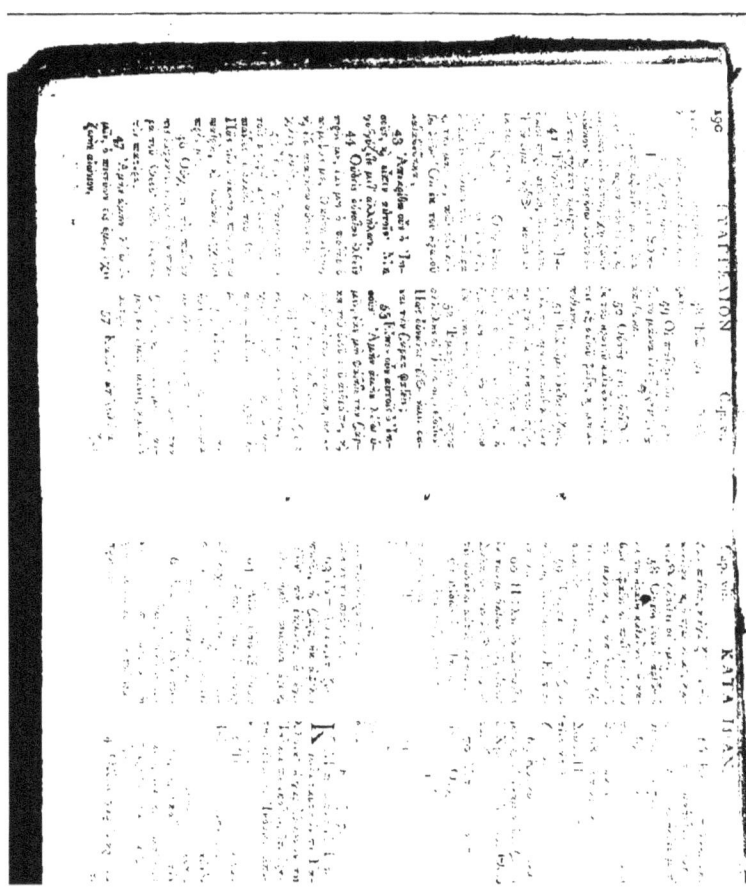

population. As time went on the Jews lost command of the Hebrew language and required a translation of their sacred books into Greek. The men who met this want differed very much in knowedge and skill, were of an indeterminate number, and of different periods, beginning the work at the time of Ptolemy Philadelphus and ending it about 150 B. C. The Pentateuch is much more carefully translated than the rest of the Bible. Books now considered apocryphal were included in the canon. The Septuagint was used by the Jews until the second century of the Christian era, when they reverted to the Hebrew. It was also, no doubt, used by the Apostles and by the Church Fathers, who refer to it under the name of "Vulgata."

TARGUM OR ARAMEAN TRANSLATION OF THE OLD TESTAMENT. Parallel edition of the Pentateuch with the Hebrew text and various Hebrew commentaries, Vienna, 1859.—Targum, which means translation, is a name specifically given to the Aramean versions. They are supposed to owe their origin to the disuse of the Hebrew tongue by exiles in Babylon. They were at first oral, and arose from the custom of having the law read in Hebrew and then rendered by the official translator (*Meturgeman*, English dragoman) into Aramean. The best Targum is that which passes under the name of Onkelos, who lived about 70 A. D. It is, however, generally assumed that, in its present shape at least, it was produced in the third century A. D. in Babylonia. That ascribed to Jonathan ben Uziel, which originated in the fourth century A. D. in Babylon and is only extant on the Prophets, is more in the nature of an homiletic paraphrase, while the so-called Jerusalem Targum ("Pseudo-Jonathan") was probably not completed till the seventh century.

FACSIMILE OF MANUSCRIPTS OF THE SEPTUAGINT, ascribed to 300 A. D.—The original is an Egyptian papyrus now at Vienna. It consists of sixteen sheets written on both sides, and contains the greater part of Zechariah from the fourth chapter and parts of Malachi. It is written in uncial characters (capitals) and contains no divisions between the words.

FACSIMILE OF THE CODEX VATICANUS, containing the Old and New Testaments, in six volumes. Rome, 1868-1881.—The Codex Vaticanus, so called from the fact that it is preserved in the Vatican at Rome, is the best and oldest Biblical manuscript now known. It is written in Greek, in uncial characters, and was probably the work of two or three scribes in Egypt during the fourth century. The original is probably the most valuable treasure of the Vatican Library. It was brought to Rome by Pope Nicholas V in 1448. The manuscript is not quite complete; there are a few gaps in the Old Testament, and the New Testament ends with Hebrews ix, 14.

CODEX SINAITICUS. Facsimile edition, St. Petersburg. Four volumes, 1862.—The Codex Sinaiticus was discovered in 1859 by Constantine Tischenforf in the Convent of St. Catharine at the foot of Mount

Sinai. It was transferred to Cairo, then to Leipsic, and later to St. Petersburg, where it is preserved in the Imperial Library. His text was printed in Leipsic from types especially cast in imitation of the original and published at St. Petersburg at the expense of Czar Alexander II. The original is on parchment, written in uncial characters, four columns to a page, and forty-eight lines on a page. It dates from the middle of the fourth century. It contains the greater part of the Old Testament and the whole of the New Testament. Four different scribes were employed in its writing.

CODEX ALEXANDRINUS. Printed in type to represent the original manuscript. London, 1816.—This facsimile version of the Alexandrian or Egyptian text of the Bible appeared in 1816 in four volumes, Volumes I-III containing the Old Testament and Volume IV the New Testament. It contains the whole Bible, with the exception of a few parts. The original manuscript was presented to King Charles I by Sir Thomas Roe, from Cyril Lucar Patriarch, of Constantinople. It was transferred to the British Museum in 1753. It is written on parchment in uncials, without division of chapters, verses, or words. Tradition places the writing of this manuscript in the fourth century, but it is now generally assumed to date from the fifth century.

THE VULGATE OR LATIN BIBLE.—The Vulgate goes back to a Latin translation made from the Septuagint, in North Africa, in the second century, and known as the *Vetus Latina* or "Old Latin." A revised form of this translation was current in Italy toward the end of the fourth century, and was known as the Itala or "Italic." The present version, however, is due to St. Jerome (Hieronymus), and was made by him in Bethlehem between 383 and 404 A. D. It was for a long time the Bible of the Western Church and of a large part of the Eastern Church. St. Jerome began the revision of the Old Testament with the book of Psalms, of which he produced three copies known as the Roman, Gallican, and Hebrew Psalters. But of the rest of the Old Testament he made a new translation from the original Hebrew, with which he was well acquainted. The translation is commonly called the Vulgate, a name which was originally given to the Septuagint. It is still in use by the Roman Catholic Church. It was printed by Gutenberg between 1450 and 1455, being the first important specimen of printing with movable types.

SYRIAC OLD TESTAMENT. Edited by S. Lee and printed at London, 1823.—The oldest Syriac version of the Bible is the Peshitta ("correct" or "simple"), the most accurate of the ancient translations. It is referred to in the Commentaries of Ephraim the Syrian, in the fourth century, and was already at that time an old book.

The whole translation was made from the Hebrew, but the translators were free in their renderings, and seem also to have been acquainted with the Septuagint.

SYRIAC NEW TESTAMENT.—Printed at Hamburg, 1664.

ARABIC BIBLE.
Cairo, Egypt.
Cat. No. 155066, U.S.N.M. Deposited by Dr. Cyrus Adler.

COPTIC NEW TESTAMENT.—Manuscript of the seventeenth century, Cairo, Egypt. Coptic was the language of the Egyptian Christians. It is a development from the ancient hieroglyphic language, with an admixture of Greek words, and continues to the present day to be used in the services of the Christian Church in Egypt. There were differences in the dialects spoken in different parts of the country, and so there are three Egyptian translations of the Bible—the Thebaic or Sahidic, the Memphitic or Bahiric, commonly called the Coptic, and the Bashmuric. They all probably date from the second century and are made after the Septuagint. The present manuscript contains St. Mark in the Bahiric dialect.

ETHIOPIC VERSION OF THE BIBLE.—Photograph of original Bible, preserved in the United States National Museum. This copy was obtained from King Theodore, of Abyssinia, by Lord Napier, and by him presented to General Grant. The Ethiopic version was made from the Septuagint in the fourth century, probably by Frumentius, the apostle of Ethiopia. It has forty-six books in all, containing, in addition to the Canon, a large number of Apocryphal books.

ARABIC VERSION OF SAADIA GAON.—In Hebrew characters. The Pentateuch, edited by J. Derenbourg, Paris, 1893. Saadia Gaon was born at Fayum, A. D. 892, and died in 942. His translation of the Bible is rather a paraphrase, and has a high exegetical value.

ARABIC BIBLE.—Manuscript. (See plate 44.) Complete Old Testament, neatly written and well preserved. Dated by scribe 1560, A. D. Cairo, Egypt.

ARABIC NEW TESTAMENT.—Contains the Epistles and Acts, the last five verses of the Acts wanting. Sixteenth century, Cairo, Egypt.

MODERN TRANSLATIONS OF THE BIBLE.

THE NEW TESTAMENT, TRANSLATED BY JOHN WYCLIFFE about 1380; printed from a contemporary manuscript by William Pickering, London, 1848. John Wycliffe was born in Yorkshire about 1320. He studied at Baliol College, Oxford, and was for some time master of that college. He became later rector of Lutterworth, in Leicestershire, and was the foremost leader of the reform party. He died in 1384. About 1380 he undertook, with the assistance of some of his followers, especially Nicholas Hereford, the translation of the entire Bible into English from the Latin of the Vulgate. It was the first complete English Bible. His translation was, after his death, revised by one of his adherents. The present copy is assumed to represent the first version prepared by Wycliffe himself, or at least under his supervision.

TYNDALE'S NEW TESTAMENT. Facsimile by F. Fry.—William Tyndale was born between 1484 and 1486 in Gloucestershire. He was educated at Oxford and afterwards at Cambridge. He went to Hamburg and later joined Luther at Wittenberg, where he finished the translation of the New Testament into English. The first edition was issued in 1525. It was the first English translation made from the Greek, and it became the basis of all subsequent ones. It was also the first part of the Scriptures printed in the English language. In 1530 the translation of the Pentateuch was issued. His English style was very good and was largely retained in the Authorized version. His translation was condemned by the English bishops, and was ordered to be burned. Tyndale was strangled for heresy at Antwerp in 1536, and his body burned.

THE GOTHIC AND ANGLO-SAXON GOSPELS, with the versions of Wycliffe and Tyndale. Arranged by Rev. Joseph Bosworth, London, 1865.—The Gothic version was made in the fourth century by Bishop Ulfilas, born 318 A. D., died about 381. It is said to have been a complete version, with the exception of the Book of Kings. It was probably completed about 360 A. D. Only fragments are preserved in the so-called Codex Argenteus, or "Silver Book," in the library of the University of Upsala, Sweden. The Anglo-Saxon version was begun by King Alfred, who translated the Psalms in the ninth century. The translation now extant dates to the tenth century.[1]

COVERDALE'S BIBLE. Reprint by Baxter, 1838.—Miles Coverdale was born at Coverham, in the North Riding of Yorkshire, 1488. He died at Geneva in 1569. His Bible was issued October 4, 1535, being the first complete Bible printed in the English language. It was not translated from the original tongues, but was based chiefly on the Latin version and on Luther's Bible. It was undertaken at the wish of Thomas Cromwell, Earl of Essex, and dedicated to Henry VIII.

THE GENEVAN VERSION. Folio edition, printed at London, 1597.—This translation was made by English exiles during the reign of Mary, who took up their residence at Geneva. William Whittingham acted as editor, and his assistants were Thomas Cole, Christopher Goodman, Anthony Gilby, Thomas Sampson, and Bishop Coverdale. Some add John Knox, John Bodleigh, and John Pullain, and state that the translators consulted Calvin and Beza. The first edition was printed at Geneva in 1560. It was printed at the expense of John Bodley, father of the founder of the Bodleian Library in Oxford. It was the most popular Bible until superseded by the Authorized version, and was that brought to America by the Pilgrim Fathers. The division of chapters into verses, which had been introduced by Whittingham, from Stephanus's edition of 1551, was here for the first time adopted for the English Bible. The text of the Bible is accompanied by explanatory comments on the margin. It is sometimes called the "Breeches" Bible because of the substitution in Genesis iii, 7, of the rendering "breeches" for "aprons" of the other English version.

KING JAMES OR AUTHORIZED VERSION. Folio edition, printed at London by Robert Barker, 1613.—The preparation of a new English Bible was decided upon at a conference held at Hampton Court January

---

[1] For Wycliffe's and Tyndale's translations see above.

16 and 18, 1604. In that year King James I issued a commission to fifty-four eminent divines to undertake the work. It was not begun, however, until 1607, when seven of the original number had died. The forty-seven survivors were divided into six committees, two sitting at Oxford, two at Cambridge, and two at Westminster. In 1610 their work was completed, and then revised by a committee of six. Although universally known as the Authorized version, no record, either ecclesiastical or civil, has ever been found of such authorization. The first edition was printed by Robert Barker in 1611.

THE REVISED VERSION.—The increased knowledge concerning the original texts of the Scriptures, especially of the Greek New Testament, which resulted from the discovery of old manuscripts led to the desire for a revision of the Authorized version which was based upon the received text of Erasmus and Stephanus and exhibited many discrepancies from the emended original text. Such a revision was early advocated by men like Bishop Ellicott, Archbishop Trench, and Dean Alford. Efforts were also made from time to time in the House of Commons to have a royal commission appointed. In 1870 the upper house of the Canterbury Convocation, on the motion of Bishop Wilberforce, took the subject in hand and instituted the proceedings which finally secured the accomplishment of the work. In 1871 an American committee of cooperation was organized. The New Testament was completed in 1881 and the Old Testament in 1885.

PARALLEL NEW TESTAMENT. Revised version and Authorized version. (Seaside Library.) The Revised version of the New Testament appeared in England May 17, 1881, and in America May 20, 1881. The first half of the parallel Testament appeared in New York May 21 and the second half May 23.

THE NEW TESTAMENT, translated by Constantine Tischendorf, Leipzig, 1869. Volume 1000, Tauchnitz series.—This translation was based on the labors of Tischendorf in revising the Greek text, largely due to his discovery of the Sinaitic Codex. It points out many errors in the Authorized version, and undoubtedly paved the way for the Revised version.

LUTHER'S BIBLE. German translation, made by Martin Luther. Edition of 1554.—The New Testament appeared in 1522 and the Old Testament in parts between 1523 and 1532. The complete Bible appeared in 1534. Previous to Luther's version there were in use at least ten distinct German versions, literal translations of the Latin Bible. Luther worked from the original tongues, and yet succeeded in giving the Bible a real German dress and a style that would appeal to German readers. Luther's translation was of prime importance in assisting the progress of the Reformation, and is also the foundation of the German literary dialect.

SPANISH OLD TESTAMENT. Amsterdam, Holland, 1661 A. D. (5421 A. M.).—The first edition of this translation was printed in the middle of the sixteenth century. It bears the title "The Bible in the Spanish language, translated word for word from the Hebrew, examined by the Inquisition, with the privilegium of the Duke of Ferrara." It is therefore generally known as the Ferrara Bible. The copies of this translation are divided into two classes—one appropriate for the use of the Jews, the other suited to the purposes of the Christians. The translation is extremely literal, and the translator has indicated with an asterisk the words which are in Hebrew equivocal, or capable of different meanings.

ELIOT'S INDIAN BIBLE. (See plate 45.) Facsimile reprint. Washington, D. C., 1890.—John Eliot, "the apostle of the Indians," was born in England in 1604 and received his education at Cambridge. In 1631 he removed to America and settled at Roxbury, Massachusetts, as minister, where he remained until his death, in 1690. He became interested in the conversion of the Indians of New England, whom he believed to be the descendants of the lost tribes of Israel, and determined to give them the Scriptures in their tribal tongue, which was the Natick dialect. He completed the translation of the New Testament in 1661 and that of the entire Bible in 1663. It was printed in Cambridge, Massachusetts, by Samuel Green and Marmaduke Johnson, "ordered to be printed by the Commissioners of the United Colonies in New England, At the Charge, and with the Consent of the Corporation in England For the Propagation of the Gospel amongst the Indians in New England."

Eliot's Indian Bible was the first ever printed in America, and the entire translation is stated to have been written with one pen. Eliot also published an Indian grammar and a number of other works, mostly relating to his missionary labors. The Natick dialect, in which the translation of the Bible was made, is now extinct.

MINIATURE BIBLE.—The smallest complete edition printed from type. Version of 1611.

CROMWELL'S SOLDIER'S POCKET BIBLE. Facsimile reprint. Compiled by Edmund Calamy and issued for the use of the army of the Commonwealth, London, 1643.—It has frequently been stated that every soldier in Cromwell's army was provided with a pocket Bible, and it was supposed that an especially small copy was used. In 1854 the late George Livermore, of Cambridgeport, Massachusetts, discovered that the Bible which Cromwell's soldiers carried was not the whole Bible, but the soldier's pocket Bible, which was generally buttoned between the coat and the waistcoat, next to the heart. It consists of a number of quotations from the Genevan version (all but two from the Old Testament) which were especially applicable to war times. Only two copies of the original of this work are known to be in existence—one in America and the other in the British Museum. The work was reissued in 1693 under the title "The Christian Soldier's Penny Bible." The only copy known to be extant is in the British Museum.[1]

---

[1] From the Bibliographical Introduction.

THE
HOLY BIBLE
CONTAINING THE
OLD TESTAMENT
AND THE *NEW*

Tranflated into the

INDIAN LANGUAGE

AND

Ordered to be Printed by the *Commiffioners of the United Colonies* in *NEW-ENGLAND*,

At the Charge, and with the Confent of the

CORPORATION IN ENGLAND

For the Propagation of the Gofpel amongft the Indians in New-England.

CAMBRIDGE:

Printed by *Samuel Green* and *Marmaduke Johnfon*.

MDCLXIII.

TITLE PAGE OF ELIOT'S INDIAN BIBLE.

HIEROGLYPHIC BIBLE. (See plate 46.) Published by Joseph Avery, Plymouth; printed by George Clark & Co., Charleston, 1820.—A number of hieroglyphic Bibles have been printed in America, the first being that of Isaiah Thomas, at Worcester, Massachusetts, in 1788. Words in each verse are represented by pictures, the whole being designed "to familiarize tender age in a pleasing and diverting manner with early ideas of the Holy Scriptures."[1]

BISHOP ASBURY'S TESTAMENT, with hundreds of the texts for his sermons marked in his own handwriting.—Francis Asbury, born in Staffordshire 1745, died in Virginia 1816, was the first bishop of the Methodist Church ordained in America. He was sent as a missionary by John Wesley in 1771, and in person organized the work of his denomination in the entire eastern portion of the United States, performed the first ordination in the Mississippi Valley, and in 1784 founded the first Methodist college.

THOMAS JEFFERSON'S BIBLE, consisting of texts from the Evangelists, historically arranged.—This book bears the title, "The life and morals of Jesus of Nazareth, extracted textually from the gospels, in Greek, Latin, French, and English." Four versions were employed. The passages were cut out of printed copies and pasted in the book. A concordance of the texts is given in the front and the sources of the verses in the margins. The section of the Roman law under which Jefferson supposed Christ to have been tried is also cited. All of these annotations, as well as the title page and concordance, are in Jefferson's own handwriting. Two maps, one of Palestine and another of the ancient world, are pasted in the front. Jefferson long had the preparation of this book in mind. On January 29, 1804, he wrote from Washington to Dr. Priestley: "I had sent to Philadelphia to get two Testaments (Greek) of the same edition, and two English, with a design to cut out the morsels of morality and paste them on the leaves of book." Nearly ten years later (October 13, 1813), in writing to John Adams, he stated that he had for his own use cut up the gospels "verse by verse" out of the printed book, arranging the matter which is evidently His (Christ's). In the same letter he describes the book as "the most sublime and benevolent code of morals which has ever been offered to man."

---

[1] The American editions are not described in W. L. Clouston's splendid work on Hieroglyphic Bibles.

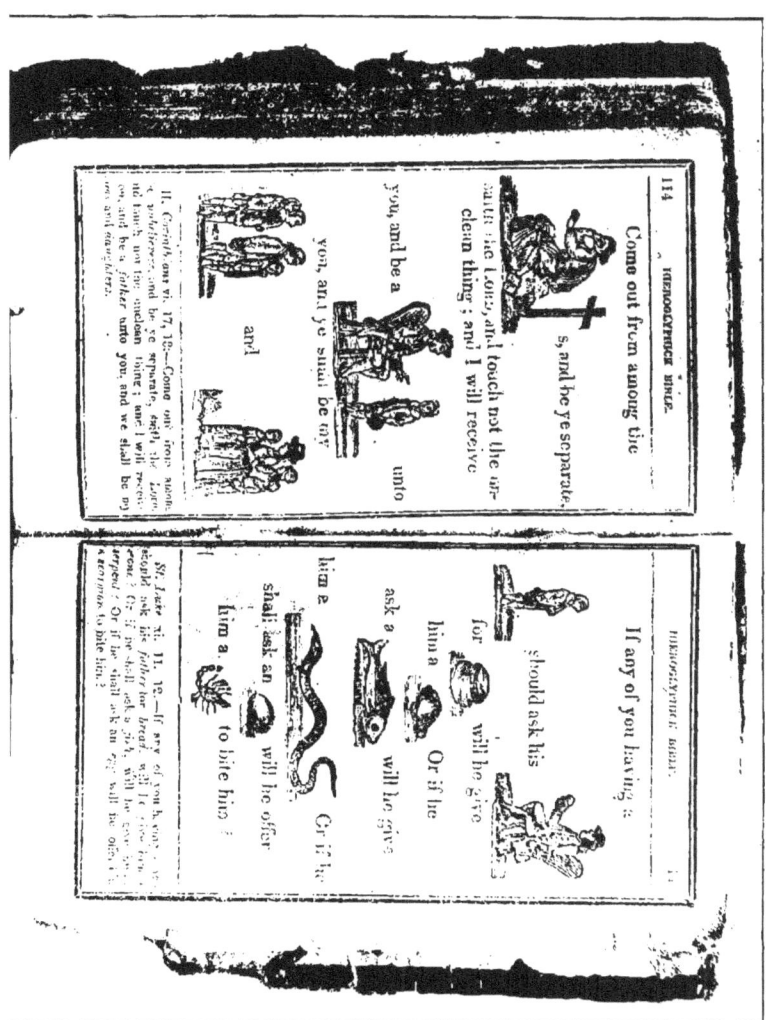

www.ingramcontent.com/pod-product-compliance
Lightning Source LLC
Chambersburg PA
CBHW020240170426
43202CB00008B/157